About

Magenta Pixie is a channel for the higher ... known as 'The White Winged Collective Consciousness of Nine'. The transmissions she receives from 'The Nine' have reached thousands of people worldwide via the extensive video collection on her YouTube channel. She has worked with people from all over the world as an intuitive consultant and ascension/consciousness coach. Magenta lives in the New Forest, UK.

Visit Magenta Pixie online at www.magentapixie.com

Also by Magenta Pixie

~ Books ~

Masters of the Matrix: Becoming the Architect of Your Reality and Activating the Original Human Template

Divine Architecture and the Starseed Template: Matrix Memory Triggers for Ascension

The Infinite Helix and the Emerald Flame: Sacred Mysteries of Stargate Ascension

The Black Box Programme and the Rose Gold Flame as Antidote: How to shield yourself from chemtrails, 5G, EMFs and other energetic warfare through alchemical unification

~ MP3 Guided Meditation Collections ~

Gateways Within

Euphoric Voyage

Sacred Quest

Elemental Dream

Cover design by Daniel Saunders and Imogen Scannell

Author photograph by Oliver McGuire of Visual Logistics

Print Edition 1, 2020

ISBN: 9798603901749

White Spirit Publishing

www.magentapixie.com

enquiries: magenta.pixie@mail.com

The information within this book is given as part of the reader's quest for spiritual enlightenment and well-being, presented from the author's personal experience and perspective.

The suggestions and advice given within this material are not to be taken as, or instead of, medical advice or as diagnosis of any kind.

The author assumes no responsibility for direct or indirect consequences arising from following this material.

The author suggests that if a change in diet or lifestyle is undertaken after inspiration from reading this book, then a fully trained medical professional, functional medicine doctor or holistic nutritionist should be consulted before embarking on any of these changes.

In no way may this text be construed as encouraging or condoning any harmful or illegal act. In no way may this text be construed as able to diagnose, treat, cure or prevent any disease, injury, symptom or condition.

Named individuals used throughout this text as examples to explain concepts and situations are fictitious. Any similarity to any persons, living or deceased, is purely coincidental.

Lessons from a Living Lemuria

Balancing Karma through Nutrition for Ascension

Magenta Pixie

This book is dedicated to my beloved husband, my children and my grandchildren.

Daniel, Alex, Abby, Rosie, Ollie, Christa, Gracie, Imogen, Riley, Rody and Elora (and any grandchildren yet to come).

...and to all lightwarriors, dreamweavers and positively polarised starseeds everywhere!

Contents

Acknowledgements

Andrew Cutler, Sharon Lewendon, Gemma McGuigan, Lesley Boyd, Dee Taylor-Mason and Dawn Holliday.

Special thanks always to my patient partner for your continuous support in life, work and play - Daniel Saunders.

Not forgetting my granddaughter Imogen Rose Scannell for assisting with the artwork for the cover. Thank you!

"Dance For Me" by Magenta Pixie

Nine white angels responding to your quest,
Guiding you through the timeline that's the best.
Should we eat deer, fish or fowl?
The answer lies with the wise old owl.

Dance for me, starseed, so I can see,
If you will assist the world to be free.
The lightworker's path is the soul's current fashion,
The keycode of choice, this time, is compassion.

From the farthest reaches of all creation,
Beyond the 'Lord Sol', he is pure emanation,
Lies a cosmic rainbow to behold,
And found beyond is the pot of gold.

Eat of the fruit of every tree,
So that you may have true eyes to see.
Discover that which shall take you higher,
The sacred compound that of 'blue starphire'.

You shall find this if you look,
It is presented in this book.
In many places does it hide,
Across your world, far and wide.

Dance for me, starseed, so you can see,
How to set your people free.
For you are the warrior, you follow the quest,
You are the highest, the just and the best.

Follow your mission with an open heart,
Discover the reality of which you are part.
With the higher dimensions, you have a bond,
Memories of Lemuria, Atlantis and beyond.

So walk now into this transmission,
To our words, carefully listen.
Enter the zone, the point that is zero,
For within this story, it is you who is hero.

Introduction

Back in the summer of 2019, someone asked whether or not there is 'karma' on eating meat. Is it possible for a person to move through an ascension process and still consume animal products?

The Nine responded to this question, and I posted the question and the reply on social media. This created a flurry of responses and many more questions!

The response from the White Winged Collective Consciousness of Nine to some of these questions triggered this transmission that is "Lessons from a Living Lemuria".

In the journey of transcribing their words, I have been given visions of the breathtakingly beautiful 'world' that is Lemuria. For that reason, this transmission is dear to my heart.

You too hold these 'memories' within. I hope that the following pages will trigger and activate you into the same love and respect for the Lemurian people and way of life, that I have.

I would like to say a very special thankyou to everyone who posted questions on social media and emailed questions related to this topic. I was unable to include them all, but I picked out the questions I feel were most relevant.

Happy reading!

Magenta Pixie X

1: Karma and the Ascension Diet

What food should we eat in order to reach enlightenment and go through ascension? Do we get karma if we eat animal products and should we be vegan?

Before we respond to your quests, we shall present a brief overview of the force within your universal structure that you name as 'karma'. Within your Bible, it does say "an eye for an eye" and "a tooth for a tooth" but this does not mean that there shall be revenge or consequence in the form of punishment. This explains simply a vibrational match. This is more akin to that which you know as 'the law of magnetic attraction' which is manifested upon your planet within your physical laws as a gravitational field.

In truth this field is a living, intelligent vibration yet one could also see this as a river, if you will, pulsating with magnetic waters. That which you do, think, put out, speak or act presents as an attracting force and this river of magnetic waters is attracted to that force. The matching cosmic material, perhaps known better to you as a plasma within a morphogenetic field, creates a pre-matter blueprint as a copy match to the force (that which you think, put out, speak or act). This force and its pre-matter attraction, perhaps best described to you as 'cause and effect', is instantaneous from our perspective. Yet from your perspective it takes on a linear quality and the magnetic reaction from the original force of attraction is not manifested within matter immediately or simultaneous to the original force. In a clear, ascending, activated aware individual it can be and this is occurring upon your planet in your now. Yet for the majority of third dimensional individuals upon your planet, there is a delay between the original force and the magnetic reaction. This is that which you may call accrued or accumulated karma. Yet in truth, it is the intelligence of the cosmic matrix or field that is at work here as you create your own reality. Your level of awakening, awareness and activation affects the experience of the magnetic attraction meaning that each individual experiences what you call 'karma' differently.

Karma is not a judgement, a punishment or anything that should create shame within the recipient. It is not literal in the sense that whatever you shall do, you shall then have this exact act done to you. Many perceive this to mean that if you are the perpetrator, you shall then become the victim in the exact same way. This is a literal interpretation and a metaphor. The truth here is energetic match, not physical interpretation. This can only be seen by those who have eyes into the antimatter realities, not just the realities of matter. The pineal gland activations shall show you these living blueprints if you stand in energetic and activated balance within all your chakra systems.

That which you call 'karma' is simply the law of your universe. It is that which is magnetic polarity, striving for individual and thus planetary and cosmic balance. It is not that which you are given as in a 'gold star if you are good' or 'reduction in a point system if you are bad'. It is not outside of you. It is part of you. It is the method or substance that the architect chose to be the means in which his/her children should remember that they are the architect. It is a memory activation tool.

You may perceive this as lessons, repeated universal teachings that come forward in many forms until you finally learn the lesson. Indeed, this is an accurate presentation of the experience. Yet in truth, what you are doing here is seeing yourself, knowing yourself and balancing yourself. This is what we mean when we use the term 'karma'. It is neither positive or negative in the sense of bad or good. It is positive and negative only in the sense of polarity and balance. Now we have presented a most basic picture of the karmic law within your universe, we may respond to your quests.

What food should we eat in order to reach enlightenment and go through ascension?

There is no 'should' here. Ascension has many stages and one can move through an 'ascension experience' regardless of dietary consumption. However, if one wishes to move through a fully aware ascension process in the most aligned way available to you at this time, which is that which we call 'accelerated' or 'stargate' ascension, one would need to have moved to that stage of mastery achieved by the indigenous peoples which is akin to being 'karma-free'.

One needs to be as 'light' as possible. The way forward here (if it is your calling and your desire) is to follow a predominantly plant-based way of eating.

Consuming small amounts of sustainably raised animal flesh (specifically seafoods) or animal products (eggs and dairy) eaten infrequently would not affect this stargate ascension process.

However, if a large amount of animal flesh - even sustainably raised seafoods - is eaten, then these codes tie you, or bind you into the physical dimension (or in the case of seafoods, the astral dimensions).

This is likely to affect your ability to raise in frequency high enough to reach full, free, fifth dimensional energy or what we may call 'permanent residence in the New Earth' (or permanent fifth strand activation).

Do we get karma if we eat animal products and should we be vegan?

Again, there is no 'should'. If you become plant-based/vegan because you think you should do so in order to ascend, yet you are miserable because you are not eating meat, than this can lower your light quotient even more than the consuming of the animal flesh.

Each case is different and each person is so very unique. We give here a guideline structure in a generalised sense, there is always exception to the rule when it comes to nourishment.

Having said that, animals raised through a lifetime of suffering and animals who have their lives taken through suffering hold a very high fear vibration within their flesh/milk/eggs. This *will* affect the human individual. In order to go through any kind of ascension, one must upgrade the animal flesh and products one consumes to ethically and naturally raised sources.

Consuming the flesh of animals who have suffered will place those fear codes into the matrix field of the individual. These fear codes are literal chemicals created by adrenaline caused through extreme fear. The attracting force to this is a service-to-self force. The mass suffering of animals and animal products then fed to the human population is a major part of the hijacking of humanity. An aspect of that which we call 'the black box programme'.

Ascension is possible when consuming animal flesh but *only* if that animal has lived a natural life and has consumed a species specific diet.

How long does one need to have maintained a strictly vegan diet in terms for karma accrued with early unconscious animal consumption to clear?

Firstly, may we say that unconscious animal consumption is 'less than' (we speak here in metaphor for as we have said there is no scale, this is simply a match to wherever you are - a mirror showing yourself to self) conscious animal consumption when aware of karmic energetic and suffering upon your planet.

Yet even less than this is conscious animal consumption when ritualised in ceremony and gratitude, following the harmonious living as the indigenous peoples. For they stand in mastery of this sacrifice. Yet in all these there are karma, for karma is part of living within the physical dimension until one reaches mastery within the balance of cause and effect.

They are then said to be 'karma-free'. Even then, this is not the case. It is more the case that it is instant balancing of the scales and living within a zero-point field, rather than a linear polarity field. Ascension, if you will, and the one who balances the karmic energetic instantaneously is the 'ascended master on Earth'.

When one becomes fully plant-based in their eating habits and thus takes the label that you refer to that is 'vegan' upon your planet, one must also hold the compassion for life and the desire to inflict as little suffering as possible within this mindset. The *intention* is everything here. The action of being the vegan through dietary means and lifestyle is the manifestation to the intention. If the intention is pure and focused then the switch from creating karma from animal consumption into freedom from the creation of that karma is instantaneous. It matters not, therefore if one has been vegan for one hour, one day, one year or one decade if the intention is pure and focused.

If one becomes vegan in lifestyle but does not hold the purity of intention to match the action then the accumulation of previous act, as in the consuming of animal flesh and by-product, may remain as a geometric frequency code within the matrix fields of that individual. However, the new action which is the consumption of only plants, also sits as a code within the matrix fields creating a mixed vibration. The karma to this is therefore a 'mixed karma' if you will (both negative and positive experience as the effect to the original cause). Therefore there shall be a linear time period whereby the karma accrued from consuming animals catches up with the new karma which is the consumption of plants. The amount of time it takes to clear that accrued karma will depend entirely upon the vibrational frequency and the individualised matrix codes of that individual.

What are some ways to honour the plants we consume to maintain lowest levels of karma/highest vibrations possible while we still choose/need to eat plants at all?

The most aligned ways to honour both plants and animals is to care for them. Therefore if you raise your own animals and plant your own plants, these will be the most aligned ways to honour them. The emotions are compassion and gratitude.

Plants are to be lovingly removed from their bush, tree or grounded state and to have thoughts sent to them of love and gratitude for the nourishment they offer. Karmic energy is balanced very quickly when consuming plants for this is directly connected to the level of the desire and will to live. This is why no amount of blessing, prayer, ritual or ceremony when taking the life of an animal can ever be balanced instantaneously. However, the overall karma of the individual can be balanced simultaneously if one follows the indigenous mastery of living in harmony with the Earth. This would mean little animal flesh or by-product is consumed within the overall diet, if a spiritual enlightenment is a goal that runs alongside the desire to live in strength and health within the physical density of Earth. We might add that *full* enlightenment has been achieved by very few indigenous masters due to the heaviness of the eating of animal flesh. However, degrees of mastery have been attained such as the ability to carry memory through death into future physical incarnations. They knew that their destiny was to remain upon a physical incarnational wheel or cycle, if you will.

The ascension and most especially the 'accelerated' or 'stargate' ascension is very different, for you are moving beyond the third density cycle and need to create the blue starphire, light speed momentum in order to achieve this. This cannot be achieved at this level by an individual still consuming animal flesh or by-product on a regular basis.

Land animal meat, eggs and dairy hold the codes for the third dimension.

Sea animal meat and eggs hold the codes for the fourth dimension.

Therefore those eating a plant-based plus seafood diet will have a higher vibrational frequency than the land animal eaters in most cases. There are variations to overall frequency.

Just as there are those who are not physically ready to become eaters of light and need no solid food, so too are there those who are not physically ready to become eaters of only plants.

If you are not eating according to your vibrational frequency then deficiencies in chemicals and codes needed for life can occur.

Therefore it is important for you to understand that we are not saying you should give up the consumption of animal flesh and animal by-product. We are simply showing you the way forward into stargate ascension, which is a journey, and there are specific stages within that journey.

The way forward therefore at this time for you, is conscious or intuitive eating. If you are drawn towards eating only plants, then follow this. If you strongly feel that eating animal flesh or animal products is right for you at this time, then follow this. This does not mean you will not attain stargate ascension for eventually, as you move forward in your ascension journey, you will naturally be led or guided by your intuition or higher guidance structure towards that which is right for you to consume. The karmic energies will balance themselves for you individually as you raise the light quotient within. The first stage of awakening when it comes to food and nourishment is the awareness of where the food comes from and how it is created. You will therefore naturally move away from the processed, chemically-laden, man-made foods and the factory farmed animal flesh and by-products that are produced through the suffering of the animal and the taking of their life, and you will move towards the clean, fresh and whole foods. You will move towards the ethically raised and appropriately fed animal flesh and by-products. Thus begins the first step into enlightenment and ascension, if you will, from the point of view of the energy you physically consume.

This first step can take many years and these stages or steps are not necessarily linear.

The second step would be to move away from land animal flesh and into sea animal flesh and animal by-products that are sustainably raised and humanely treated. Within this second step may be the moving away from all animal flesh entirely and the consuming of eggs and dairy products.

We may add that the consuming of conventionally raised dairy products holds a high karma in itself, even though you are not consuming the actual flesh of the animal. This is due to the fact that the infant animal has been deprived of the mother's milk, the very life force of nourishment, and to this end this amounts to the energetic of taking without permission or stealing.

The only way to consume dairy products relatively karmically-free is to raise the animal yourself and ensure that the infant animal feeds first. When the infant has had its fill then the remaining milk can be consumed in its raw state. This is then seen as an offering or a gift and is karma-free.

The same will be the case for eggs. Only when the chicken, duck or other egg-laying animal is allowed to raise some young and there are unfertilised eggs available that would not become life, then these can be consumed.

The next step would be to move into a fully plant-based or vegan lifestyle. At first this may contain the processed and the chemically-laden or man-made, but will be created from intentions to reduce suffering through compassion and love of animals. The higher vibratory state to this is the one who consumes the clean and the whole food plant-based products only.

Now if these individuals were drawn to the plant-based way of eating through their vibration matching this, through compassion and love, then these are the individuals that will be able to create the blue starphire, light speed momentum within the cellular structure of their bodies. Compassion is the code for acceleration of DNA.

The individuals who were drawn to the plant-based lifestyle through means other than compassion and love for all life, for example through health reasons or dietary challenges for amusement or experimentation, will find that the plant-based lifestyle creates within them a natural compassion and love for all life simply through the creation of a higher vibration.

It is, predominantly the *raw* plant foods that hold the codes for stargate ascension. There are many other tools for raising light within. Food and nourishment is only one part of the bigger picture. Yet your quests within this transmission are regarding karma and foodstuffs consumed for ascension, so we remain within this topic.

The next step would be to move into a liquid only diet. Humanity as a whole is not fully at this stage at this time. There are individuals who are but when it comes to the collective consciousness of humanity, particularly starseeds, the foods and nourishments eaten at this time are naturally and ethically raised animal and animal products and those following the plant-based or vegan lifestyle.

The next step is into a cellular structure whereby you would only need to consume light. This is known upon other planetary systems as 'ambrosia' or 'nectar'.

Again, this is not where humanity sits on a collective level at this time, although there are some individuals who are at this stage.

The life extension into immortality within physicality is fully engaged on a cellular level once it is ambrosia or nectar that is consumed. However, one must have enough blue starphire (light speed momentum into retained memory) to be able to sustain the physical body.

This is a solar ascension process, the seeds of which were downloaded into the receptive human psyche around the time of the 'Diamond Lion's Gate Portal' in August 2019. We say here 'seeds' which will draw you into the desire for raw foods, liquids and periods of fasting which are precursors to ambrosiac consumption.

You may be fully aware that the 'eating of light' (or taking the path of the breatharian) is the path for you *at some point.* You may even have memory of eating this way in a past incarnation (which is actually the same thing as you 'going to be eating this way in the future' for you are moving within spiral formation which causes you to come full circle on a soul level).

We do not recommend you move into this breatharian lifestyle until you have followed the required steps and initiations which are beyond the scope of this transmission (although the initiations for this are available on your planet through scribes other than our conduit).

Disclaimer

The breatharian lifestyle can be dangerous for a human entity who has not reached the specific light quotient necessary for this. As we have said, this is NOT where the collective consciousness of humanity is at the point of this transmission. We present the information only to show you a timeline of humanity's lifestyle specific to nourishment as you go through your ascension stages as a planet.

2: Animal and Plant Consciousness

I see that you are saying here that we cannot ascend if we are eating meat. This upsets me a great deal. I eat a lot of meat but I am going through an ascension process, I am in touch with my own guides and they have said I am fine to eat meat and that I can still ascend. I don't understand why you are saying all this.

It is not the case that you cannot ascend if you are eating meat. However, if the meat you are consuming is from an animal that has been factory farmed and has lived a life of suffering, then these fear codes will enter into your matrix and your physical body. This is akin to having heavy sandbags placed within the basket of your hot air balloon. If you wish your hot air balloon to 'take off' then you must throw the sandbags out.

The fear codes are service-to-self codes which anchor you into the negative polarised reality. In the physical body these fear codes can create fear, anxiety, depression, confusion, infections and disease.

Part of the lightness of polarity into the New Earth is the insertion of liberty templates into the galactic grid structure. The freedom codes that stem from these liberty templates are to be received by all life, animals as well as humans. The way to release from these fear codes is to upgrade from factory farmed animal flesh and products into sustainably raised animal flesh and their products.

This information is not delivered in order to cause upset within the starseed community. Ascension can take place when the meat consumed does not hold the fear codes within its flesh.

It is most in alignment for you to be in touch with your guidance system above all else and we would urge you to take this pillar of light, vertical axis, ascension tool into higher communication with your guidance structure. It may be that you need the animal flesh in your reality at this time, but we would invite you to consider the sustainably raised meats.

We are saying this simply because we have been asked the question. We are aware that the topic of the eating of the foodstuffs upon your planet is most contentious, shall we say? This is due to the fact that this is directly linked to your survival instincts via the base chakra. This, however, is one of the easiest streams for the service-to-self factions to hijack. Your dietary habits have been and are hijacked in every arena from information, history, medicine and then through actual toxins placed into natural foodstuffs and the creation of processed and man-made foodstuffs.

To release from this hijacking, one must consume foods closest to their origin in all respects.

When consuming animal products in balance, this needs to be done through harmonious energetic exchange. The factory farming is an extreme distortion of the harmony we speak of. This is deliberate and is a control tool alongside the hijacking of your education and health systems.

There are various stages to ascension, as we have said before.

There is partial ascension, ascension in balance and full stargate ascension, if you will. This is all akin to the different memory streams you are able to access through DNA activation.

It is simply not possible to move through ascension in balance or full stargate ascension if you are consuming factory farmed meat or animal products where suffering of the animal is involved.

Partial ascension may occur in rare cases whereby individuals are consuming factory farmed animal products. This would be the case where the degree of suffering of the animal is unknown and the individual believes the flesh to be from sustainable and ethical sources. This is extremely rare as the majority of ascending individuals will have the suffering of the animal brought to their attention at some point.

So if I upgrade all my meat products to ethically sourced and sustainably reared then can I still not go through stargate ascension?

It is highly unlikely that stargate ascension would be achieved if you are eating a lot of meat, even sustainably raised. It is possible this could occur if the only meat product you consume is wild-caught fish. However, ascension and stargate (or accelerated) ascension are metaphors for the same thing.

Stargate ascension is clear memory in balance. The DNA 'spins faster' if you will, and one has an 'easier ride'. In stargate ascension, one 'leads others' through the stargate and is able to create their own stargate at will. The practice and training for this comes from astral projection, out-of-body experience, dreamtime work, deep meditation and remote viewing or merkabah travel. Consuming land animal flesh and products holds a codex that is somewhat 'heavy'. This affects dreamtime work and out-of-body travel.

The reason for this 'heaviness' is due to the amount of desire and will the animal has to live. Even the sustainably raised animal does not wish to have its life taken. Therefore there is a 'karmic code' accrued when one consumes the animal flesh. This is simply the law of universal balance. If you take another being's life force in order to sustain your own, then there is a karmic energetic to this.

However, simply incarnating within the third dimension creates a karmic energetic in itself. The reality you exist within is set up so that you consume another being's life force in order to sustain your own. This is how your reality has been set up since the beginning of your 'known history'.

Through planetary ascension, the polarity fields are changing, they are lessening. Therefore the human vehicle and the entire human social system is changing. The idea is to create as little suffering to another being as you possibly can and to effectively create healing wherever and whenever you can.

A great many starseeds have now raised their vibration to the point where they no longer need to consume animal products in order to survive. They do not need to consume the life force of another being *in the same degree.* This does not mean you are not going through an ascension process if you eat meat, or that you cannot be a spiritual teacher or that you cannot be a healer. However, in almost all these cases you will be drawn towards or guided to a plant-heavy diet.

So what about plants? Are you not consuming another being's life force when you eat plants? Surely they have a will to live also?

This is what we mean when we say that plant-based eaters do not need to consume the life force of another being *in the same degree.*

Animals hold an individualised consciousness like humans. They have far more 'herd' or 'pack' mentality but they hold individualised consciousness. They therefore resist death. That resistance to death is in the same proportion to their will and desire to live (and thus the karma accrued by those who choose to consume them).

Plants do not hold individualised consciousness. They are a collective consciousness. They exist in multiple dimensions simultaneously. When a carrot is plucked from the ground, indeed, in that moment it does not want to cease living, yet within the collective consciousness the awareness remains for life for that carrot. The blueprint within the higher dimensions remains. These blueprints contain information. That information needs to be passed into the physical dimension in order for the entire dimension to upgrade. The being that consumes the (correctly grown) carrot (or whichever plant it may be) receives the information code. The information code is geometric language within light. It is received when the foodstuff is eaten in its raw or original state only. Due to the overall desire for lightcodes to be passed through the plant foods, there is no resistance to death. Only in that now moment as the plant moves from life to ceasing life is there a transitionary experience for the collective consciousness within the plant kingdom. Yet there is a simultaneous 'rejoicing' (if you will) as the light codes of information have been passed to another soul.

Animals that eat the raw plant foodstuffs receive the light codes. These light codes are transmuted within the animals flesh into nutrients but the information is received only by the animal.

Whilst you can access nutrients, vitamins and minerals from the consuming of animal flesh and products, there are no information codes within. The information codes are only within the plants.

When the plant 'dies' (and many are still living as they are consumed in their raw state), there is a change or shift in consciousness from one state of being to another but there is no resistance. Therefore the will or desire to live is only experienced within the plant's now moment of being alive whilst in the growing state. The karma accrued is therefore so minimal as to be almost at the 'karma-free' level, if you will.

I heard another channel say that animals know they are going to die and they freely give of themselves when they incarnate onto planet Earth. If this is true, then why would we accrue any karma for eating them?

The response to this is long and complex. We do our best to explain. The channel you heard was speaking truth, however it is not so literally interpreted. We must speak here of destiny and free will in order for you to understand and process the response to this question.

3: Destiny and Free Will Templates

in Animal Soul Groups

I heard another channel say that animals know they are going to die and they freely give of themselves when they incarnate onto planet Earth. If this is true, then why would we accrue any karma for eating them?

Firstly we would say, remember that 'karma' is a force that runs through you simply by virtue of being incarnated in physicality on planet Earth. It is not a punishment or point system.

Animals 'know' that they are 'going to die' only from the perspective of the creation of the blueprint of their experiences. The individualisation of the blueprint is much less than in a human incarnation, except in the case of domestic pets such as dogs, cats, rabbits, horses and so on that will be living in close proximity to the human family.

So there is a 'group' template for animals, created with certain individualisations. This is created prior to the animal's incarnation. This is not as a simple as 'the animal willingly gives of itself to be eaten'. This would be in direct contradiction to the will to live and the resistance to death. However, this is not to say that the incarnating animal does not 'know', on some level, its destiny (blueprint). The animal also has free will within that destiny in the shape of multiple possibilities and probability fields for the animal. The core experience is always for survival.

In a harmonious planet, the blueprint would be created for the pack, herd or group. Within that group there would be few that are 'destined' within most probable timelines for that group, to give of themselves to feed another animal or human soul. They incarnate willingly in order to experience their reality and to experience destiny and free will as a human does. From that higher perspective the soul (and the group soul) gives of their life force willingly to assist the overall planetary ecosystem based on the template of life force consuming other life force. This would be destiny, if you will.

However, that animal also incarnates with codes for free will, a core template for survival and a high will/desire to live *regardless of the blueprint of destiny from the higher level.*

From the perspective of the actual physically incarnated animal, no part of that animal knows it is going to die and freely gives of itself to feed another. The animal will fight and resist with all its might. So whilst there is truth in the comment made here, it is truth only from the higher dimensional perspective (destiny) and not from the physical perspective (free will).

Due to the fact that the indigenous masters instinctively know all this through the connected conduits that are the 'wise women' and 'wise men' of the tribes, then the animal that is going to be consumed is very carefully selected. Much ritual and divination would be done prior to the culling of that animal. The animal chosen to be the sacrifice for the indigenous tribe to consume would be called into their reality and communicated with telepathically.

Then they would be sure to call to them the animal that is the least destructive to the herd or group, such as an ageing female who can no longer bear young for the group.

With the fishing of seafood there would be similar divination but groups of fish or seafood would be taken from the sea at a time rather than an individual larger land animal.

Often the tribal peoples would live on the berries, nuts and fruits of the land until an animal actually presented itself in their path. Only then would that animal's life be taken to feed the tribe. So the precision, reverence, honour and ritual was profound and specific. This would ensure that the contract between the animals giving their lives and the humans consuming them remained intact. This would become part of what is known as the 'circle of life'.

All this, that we have just explained, occurs within a fully functioning, balanced and free-flowing, harmonious planet. This was the way for many indigenous peoples living in the past upon your planet.

However, the food systems on your planet have been hijacked. The incarnational lines of the animals have been trapped as much as the human lines have been. All this is, indeed, in the process of change. Yet for many years, animals were forced to simply reincarnate over and over again to be incarnated into the slavery system of factory farming. This is a complete distortion of the incarnational journey for these groups of animals. They are unable to 'reach' the 'place' from where they can plan a group blueprinted destiny for their incarnation as those blueprints were 'stolen' if you will. This was to use the animals to create a 'death'/'pain'/'fear toxicity' within their flesh to market and feed to the human population.

There are those upon your planet who expose the corruption of the meat, dairy and egg industry and they present to you that these corrupt industries put profit before the health of the people of Earth. This is true, yet at the topmost levels of this pyramidical structure it is not profit that drives these factions but complete control of the population and ultimately *prevention of ascension.*

This is the ultimate agenda. Prevention of the reconstruction of your DNA memory fields back into the 144 configuration of light.

The control grids, black box programmes and inverted matrix trapping systems *are* breaking down in all areas. The way to become a true indigo lightwarrior/systems buster and disrupter of this dark matrix, specific to this topic, is to cease purchasing and consuming these toxic foodstuffs that are the flesh of trapped animal souls and upgrade to consuming ethically reared and sustainably farmed animal products, or better still to become fully plant-based/vegan. You can see now why we talk of karma and how you accumulate this when you consume these factory farmed animals. You take on the codes for the dark, inverted matrix and the service-to-self structure when you consume the fear-based animal flesh.

Does it not take starseeds though to transmute this? Can we not give gratitude and thanks on a large scale and continue to eat factory farmed meat knowing we have released the animals soul through our prayers?

There is much contradiction here. We shall explain.

The majority of starseeds are following nicely aligned and activated guidance structures which are the wise knowings within or the 'voice of the DNA'.

Many of these starseeds are already drawn towards the ethically raised animal products and the vegan lifestyle. In fact, the great majority of starseeds drawn to this transmission are a match to this information simply because it is confirmation for them of their own knowings and higher guidance received.

With the knowings these starseeds have comes the determination to end the suffering of the animals on this planet that they see as their friends. To a starseed holding a vegan philosophy, it is no different to them than the thought of eating a cow, a pig, a dog or a cat. To them it is the same. Through their high level love and compassion for the animals, they are already putting out a call for assistance in the cessation of the factory farming and the cruelty the animals endure. Therefore your combined prayers of gratitude for the animals giving of themselves for your nourishment is not in alignment or in harmony with the compassionate call for the ending of their suffering.

If any starseed were to attempt to give thanks and offer prayer to the animal (and it is always good to do this even when eating factory farmed animal flesh), they would be able to feel the distortion. For what you do when you give thanks and prayer is connect telepathically with the animal as the indigenous elders did. Instead of being able to choose the animal to feed your tribe, you would be met with the dark vibration of suffering, pain, fear and death and the extremely loud and continuous cry for help from these animals and from the starseeded humans who consider them to be their friends.

Your prayers at this level will not release the animal's soul, for as we have said these are hijacked animal group souls. However, we are not saying that these animals souls cannot be released. They can. How this is done is by less and less individuals purchasing meat, dairy and eggs from the factory farmed sources. This drives trade and demand in other areas such as sustainably raised animals and plant foods. Due to the movement towards ethical foods, some animal souls are being released from these trapping systems. Yet the service-to-self groups hold on tightly to this system as they see this as a major aspect of control over humanity. You will begin to see changes in this structure as more and more people become aware and make those changes. By 2021 there will be significant change in this area. There are many starseeds who have incarnated with a core mission to assist animals and these core missions, in alignment with the ascension timeline, are coming to fruition more and more.

What about the health benefits of eating meat, fish, dairy and eggs? What if the individual needs to eat these things and they cannot access sustainably raised animal products?

We would suggest you access the best quality foods that you can. Any health benefits within these factory farmed animal products are outweighed by the toxicity within the animal's flesh and products that hold fear/pain/death codes.

Reading this is all so depressing. I am already a plant-based vegan and I don't need to be reminded of the suffering that goes on in factory farming. Is there any good news at all because it all sounds just awful to me.

Indeed, there is much 'good news' if you will. There are major changes occurring upon your planet as the liberty templates begin to be activated within the DNA. The liberty templates hold the codes for freedom, and that includes animals.

We understand that this information is difficult for a plant-based eater to hear as they hold such high compassion within their fields. The light created by the high compassion you hold translates to being easily sensitive and upset whenever you hear about the suffering of animals. The majority of starseeds are incarnated with a natural love of animals. In fact, even the starseeds still eating factory farmed meat hold love of animals. Many are not aware of the information we present here, yet we understand that many of you *are* aware. The starseed community is as a wave, with varying degrees of awareness in different subjects. Within this transmission, we are specifically responding to questions regarding karma and of the most appropriate diet for an ascending starseed.

So what is the most appropriate diet for an ascending starseed?

4: The Lemurian Diet – Back to the Garden

Each ascending soul is uniquely different and has individual needs. There is no one-size-fits-all diet, much as individuals following an aware and awakened path would like there to be. It would be so easy if one person had the answer on what is the most appropriate diet to follow.

One of the reasons you are incarnated upon this planet is for discovery. That explorer's journey, if you will, is the discovery of self and this includes your health and how to live in the healthiest possible way. Tips, tools and guides can be given but ultimately the journey into self is yours. Why? Because there is only self and that self is you.

What we can say, on a general level, is that a 'compassionate' diet is the most appropriate diet for an ascending individual. What that looks like to you, is individual and unique.

There have been many communities and cultures who have followed appropriate and optimum nutritionally sound and spiritually activating diets. We speak of diet plans followed by traditions of Ayurveda, macrobiotic, the Essenes and several Eastern societies.

Yet if we really want to look at a pure society that has existed upon your planet, we can turn to the Lemurian civilisation.

These were a harmonious, peaceful and loving people. Their diet was predominantly an uncooked diet for many years, yet powdered and crushed roots made into flatbreads of a sort were also consumed. The only animal product that was eaten was occasional fish and they were only eaten in times of scarcity (which were rare in Lemuria) or in times of illness when a deeper nourishment was needed.

The Lemurians were a water-dwelling and water-loving society. Fish and other sealife (early Earth did not have habitable land nearby to oceans at that time but there were plentiful habitable areas near to rivers and lakes) were seen as holy and they were honoured, respected and hailed as high vibrational life forms.

This dietary plan is most in alignment for ascending starseeds. The fish to be given during times of illness for nourishment is no longer viable upon your planet due to pollutions within your seas. In the Lemurian days, the fish were clean and abundant with zero toxicity or pollution. The nearest thing you would have upon your planet would be the wild salmon. Some clean sources can still be found upon your planet.

In order to mimic the Lemurian way of eating, one would bring in the sea vegetables instead of the fish if one wanted to remain plant-based and still bring in the energy of the ocean.

So what did the Lemurians eat?

Fruits, different types depending on where they were upon your planet. Many fruits they ate do not grow upon your planet any longer. Staple fruit were like a cross between a melon and a coconut, where the liquid inside the fruit could be consumed through a hole in the fruit like your coconut of today.

Yet you can easily emulate their diet today through consuming fresh fruits in their original state, unspoiled by changing the DNA of the fruit, forcing new types to grow or by spraying them with chemicals. The citrus fruits are especially helpful for the ascending starseed.

The fruit in its natural state would be the predominant diet. To emulate the very fatty fruits that the Lemurians had access to, then avocados and olives would suffice.

Vegetation was also eaten and this would be soft, green leaves. To emulate the mineral-rich leaves eaten, then including leafy greens in your diet would be in alignment.

This would be the staple for the Lemurians. They also had milk, yet this milk came from coconut-like fruits, not from animals. Drinking a good quality coconut milk would therefore match the Lemurian's way of eating.

In their society, the men ate differently to the women. They would eat more green plant materials and that which you call nuts, with an emphasis on the Brazil nut.

The females ate far more fruits and drank lots of the fruit milk.

You are moving back into a 'new Lemuria' if you will, as in the simplicity, peace, compassion, unity and love of the Lemurians with the intellectual, magickal and technological traits of the Atlanteans.

Of all the dietary plans upon your planet, the Lemurian would be the closest diet that would be most in alignment for ascending starseeds.

We would therefore say that either the plant-based vegan diet or the dairy free, egg free pescatarian diet are the closest to the Lemurian way of eating.

This would be translated (plant-based) as fruits, vegetables, sea vegetables, coconut milk, nuts, seeds, root vegetables, beans and herbs. This would be the closest to the Lemurian diet, translated into your now time.

As pescatarian, this would translate as all of the above with the addition of wild sustainably caught salmon. If animal milk is desired then goats milk is much more in harmony with the ascending light body, most especially if this is sustainably raised and freely given by the mother goat.

You said Lemurians were 'water-dwellers.' Did they actually live in the water?

Early Lemurians, yes. This is where your legends (and memories) of mermaids and mermen come from. (Yet this memory is also a coded trigger for merkabah activation.)

After many years, they migrated onto habitable land. It is the later, land-dwelling Lemurians that are the peoples we speak of when we talk about 'the Lemurian diet'.

This diet we speak of can also be found in your Bible. It is that which is called 'the Garden of Eden diet'. This is the Lemurian diet.

Then God said, "I give you every seed-bearing plant on the face of the whole earth and every tree that has fruit with seed in it. They will be yours for food."

Genesis 1:29

Can you speak more about the karma accrued with substances such as alcohol, caffeine and sugar? And then about plant-based medicines such as cannabis, peyote, mushrooms, ayahuasca and so on?

Each substance you speak of here will create an energetic match (a signature) within the individual. This is a merge between the substance and the individual, and the resulting signature for the cause and effect attraction in that individual's reality (karma) will be unique. For example, alcohol can open a gateway/portal for nefarious and lower density entities to enter and thus 'feed' from the energy system of the person drinking the alcohol. However, the individual needs to be of like-vibration to those negative entities in the first place. Therefore, two people may drink the same alcoholic substance and one opens a portal to a negative entity that then feeds from his/her energy and the other does not open the portal and remains immune from negative energetic siphoning of his/her energy field.

Therefore we must continue to generalise regarding each substance you mention.

Alcohol

This is a fermented sugar that can have both beneficial and extremely harmful causation within the physical body, depending on how it is created. The causation within the body creates the energy signature and the 'karma' thus accrued is a match to that.

For a naturally created alcohol (from fruit, seed or plant) that is ritualised, treated as sacred and used only for vision questing (through purposeful positive intentional creation) then this would accrue no karmic imbalance (other than the utilising of the life force of said fruit/plant which we have already discussed).

The man-made mass produced alcohols, laden with chemicals and additives and consumed recreationally, do create a karmic energetic. This would be akin to confusion, chaos, ill health, dumbing down of one's electrical fields, exhaustion, negative spiral reality systems (continuous bad luck) and, as we have said, the deliberate offering of oneself to be consumed by negative forces/entities/beings.

There is much we could say upon alcohol but that will digress from the cohesive, central thread of this transmission. Thus that which we have said shall suffice as it responds to your quest.

Caffeine

This is the substance that creates the 'speeding up' of energy. Leading to energetic stimulation for those who are low and weak in fire, yet leading also to chaos systems in those who already hold enough fire. There is a place for minimal use of naturally created caffeine beverages. Depending on the beverage utilised, as each contains a slightly different form of that which you call caffeine (which is an umbrella term). Healing can take place from this substance if the match is in alignment. Therefore neutral and positive 'karma' is thus created.

Like alcohol, this substance can be abused and utilised without intention, consuming that which is man-made, altered and chemically-laden. Whilst this in itself does not open a portal or gateway to negative entities, it can create chaotic patterning within cell growth and thought structure. Karma is minimal, however, for there is no 'suffering' involved as is the case with animal consumption. The karma, as energetic match, is to that which is fast-moving and out of control creating 'chaos' within one's life. This substance is therefore not recommended for ascending lightworkers unless minimal and intentionally focused regarding reason of use. The one exception is the beverage created from the leaf that results in the 'green tea'. The healing properties outweigh the chaos factor which is much smoother within the individual's physical structure. It is the choice of the ascending one as to whether they include this in their nutritional plan. For full stargate ascension, we would not recommend it. The reason being that the 'speed'/'momentum' created by the green tea substance that mimics caffeine can interfere with the building of natural light speed momentum (blue starphire). However, for ascension in balance the green tea will not affect and the karmic energetic is mostly neutral.

Sugar

When this is from the plant such as the coconut, there is minimal karma or physical effect. Small amounts can be utilised and only bring benefit or neutrality despite this being a fractionated substance. One would recommend the whole food in all cases first and foremost. The coconut sugar and good quality maple syrups hold high energy signatures and can be utilised without negative signatures being created. So, neutral and in some cases positive karmic energy.

Honey, also a sugar, is a mixed energetic and a difficult one to present regarding karma. If the honey is 'freely given' from the bees (as in the bees keep what they need to sustain the hive and the beekeeper collects the remaining as an energy exchange for caring for the hive) then the honey is karma-free.

In the majority of cases however, the honey will hold the energetic of 'stealing' and 'suffering' although this is not at the same high level as animal flesh.

Some honeys are extremely beneficial to the human body and can act as a conductor for plasmic light as the DNA activates in ascension. Therefore the ascending starseed will make the choice between karmic signature creating the match and utilising the compounds in honey (and other bee products) for the conductivity of light. There is no other natural sweetener that holds the ability to conduct the plasmic light as much as the high level raw honeys (such as manuka and others).

The milk from the coconut does also have the ability to conduct plasmic light as does transdermal magnesium (such as Himalayan sea salts that can be used within one's bathwater or the magnesium oils). So honey is not the only form of this conductive element available.

To take the 'karma' is the choice of the ascending one and will depend on the way the honey is gathered from the hive versus the need for its beneficial assistance.

The refined sugar itself is of a very low vibration. The first few boilings of the sugar cane resulting in the molasses and the blackstrap molasses is where the nutrients will be found. There is much healing to be found by consuming the blackstrap molasses in pure and clean form with neutral/positive karmic signature.

The refined part of the sugar is stripped of all its nutrients and therefore its life force and health-giving properties. The refined sugar does the opposite of conduct plasmic energy. It dims the light within and prevents the plasmic energy/light from being conducted. It is an anti-conductor.

Refined sugar itself does not open portals to negative entities as does the alcohol (the fermented version of the sugars). However, it can dim the light so much within an individual that they are always becoming a vibrational match to any 'passing negative entity' that may be around (having entered the reality through tears/rips in the timespace fabric of that particular individual's reality timeline - for example, through another individual close to them).

The vibrational match to refined sugar 'karma' is therefore 'lack of life force'. We strongly advise all ascending individuals to avoid this substance within their ascension journey.

The karmic energy is still not as high or dramatic as the consumption of animal flesh however, and ascension can take place with minimal use of refined sugar. With the higher vibratory options available then this would be the direction one would be guided towards.

In truth, no sugars are needed within the ascending individual's physical body other than the natural sugars contained within the fresh unspoiled, unaltered fruits. The waters within these fruits act as mini-conductors of plasmic light energy in themselves and they do this through cleansing the system. Opening the pathways through the body to act as conduits of light. This takes the vibration higher and higher as the light body forms.

There are two types of foodstuffs to ensure are consumed regularly in the diet, as the Lemurian races instinctively knew. One is the cleansing and clearing foodstuff (predominantly fruits) and the other is the nourishing and balancing foodstuff (predominantly vegetables).

So one is looking to be cleansed and nourished simultaneously when following the nutritional plan of choice for ascension.

Cannabis, Peyote, Mushrooms, Ayahuasca, etc

We can place these substances in one camp for general explanation, the camp we may call 'mind-altering substances'.

What we say here is very similar to that which we said for alcohol. That which is man-made, chemically created or not procured through natural means holds a dark energetic signature and therefore much karma. There is a difference between alcohol and the man-made unnatural mind-altering substances. The difference is in the weight and breadth of the energy signature. The man-made unnatural mind-altering substance holds much darker, heavier energy and therefore a substantial negative karma. In some circumstances, the negative karma is greater than even that of the factory farmed animals. This is due to 'suffering' caused in the procurement of said substances. These substances also open portals to negative lower astral forces, yet the energetic is much lower than and greater than that of the alcohol. For example, if alcohol consumption opens a portal and allows in two or three (we use metaphor here) negative entities, then the man-made unnatural substances open portals to between fifteen and several hundred negative entities. The reason for this is the deep level the

46

chemical reactions to the man-made unnatural substances stretch to. The alcohol does not touch the deep cellular aspect of the physical body in the same way as the man-made unnatural mind-altering substance.

Once the alcohol is consumed then the portal is closed, if you will. The alcohol is removed through detoxification pathways within the body. The only way a portal into the negative astral realms may remain open is if the person is continuously consuming alcohol.

With the man-made unnatural mind-altering substance, the portal remains open for much longer than the individual feels the effects for (allowing in a much larger 'group' of negative entities).

The detoxification pathways do not work in the same way on these compounds which merge with bloodstream matter. Our conduit does not have the biological understanding within her fields for the explanation of the chemical reaction here. Just know that the substance 'becomes at one' with the make-up of the individual's body. The detoxification pathways therefore do not recognise the mind-altering substance as that which needs to be detoxed from the body as they do with the alcohol. This is connected to the fact that the alcohol is a sugar molecule that triggers an insulin reaction. The mind-altering substance triggers chemical reactions that are not insulin-based.

Therefore 'karma' upon these man-made unnatural mind-altering substances is large and can affect the individual drastically.

Can an ascending individual take these substances and not open a portal?

Yes, it is possible that in rare cases they could prevent the portal from being opened. However, when we say 'rare' we mean rare. There are few that could do this. However, an ascending starseed need not be affected by the negative entities even if a portal is opened within them. The great majority of ascending individuals would not come into contact with these types of substances as this is a vibrational mismatch. Only those who are 'partially ascending' may do so.

What is 'partial ascension'?

One who ascends 'in part' (as in 'accesses higher dimensional information and true memory') whilst still holding uncleared, unknown, unresolved and buried trauma. The trauma codes may attract the mind-altering substances into the individual's reality as a vibrational match. However, even this is rare given the higher memory fields present as a mismatch.

The ascending starseed is far more likely to attract the natural mind-altering substances into their reality, such things as that which you call 'cannabis', 'peyote', 'mushrooms' and 'ayahuasca'. Whilst these can be man-made or have man-made equivalents, we speak now regarding the natural. That which grows naturally on your planet, and that which is procured with love and focused intention.

These can be used for vision questing. Triggers in and of themselves for awakening. To be used as a spiritual tool for divination, spell casting, pineal gland activation, astral travel, deep meditation and deep insightful magical work and manifestation. This includes healing, balance and all that which ascending individuals are doing naturally.

These substances only work up to a point. Until that point they are useful and if procured with care, grace and gratitude, they hold neutral and positive karma. However once that point is passed, the substance begins to work negatively for the individual. The fear-based anxiety pathways are triggered.

The point is that which is no longer a vibrational match.

Many newly awakened individuals are a vibrational match to these tools. These plant compounds that hold mind-altering substances are major portals of awakening, indeed opening portals of light into higher realms. The vibrational match to cause and effect being most positive.

However, once an individual has naturally reached these levels on their own (creating their own natural mind-altering substance within) then they no longer need the assistance of 'plant spirits'. It may take several lifetimes to get to the point where you move beyond the need for plant spirit assistance, yet this is where the majority of you are now. You do not need the plant spirit assistance as a substance you take into your body. The reason for this is because you are creating your own inner mind-altering substance (known as 'manna', 'ormus', 'inner gold', 'ambrosia', 'rose pink golden liquid', 'Kundalini phire' or indeed 'the Holy Grail'). When you have this inner gold (which in composition is almost identical to that which you know as 'dimethyltryptamine' or 'DMT'), if you also take the plant spirit substance, you then have 'too much.'

The inner golden substance creates within you 'blue starphire' which is light speed momentum needed for accelerated or stargate ascension. It is created in the exact correct amounts.

If you also consume the plant spirit molecules, you will create 'too much' blue starphire and this leads to burn out. You burn out and are unable to raise the momentum for stargate ascension.

The correct amount of blue starphire creates a smooth lightness with just enough fire for 'lift off' if you will.

The plant spirits are tools into the creation of blue starphire. But once you are creating the blue starphire on your own then you thank the plant spirit for its assistance, but you realise it is no longer needed.

So you can see, everything you consume within you has some kind of reaction that you know as 'cause and effect' or 'karma'. A unique energetic signature is thus created betwixt your energy signature and that of the substance or foodstuff you consume.

The Lemurians knew all this instinctively. Following the Lemurian diet, as best as one can mimic it within your modern-day now moment, is absolutely in perfect alignment for your ascending light body at this time.

6: The Lord of Karma

Can you please speak about B12? You are advocating a plant-based diet for ascension, but without B12 you can run into problems and you cannot get B12 from a plant-based diet.

That which you speak of was abundant upon your planet in the soils and in the environment. Yet due to plundering of Earth's mineral-rich soils and the spraying of the black box programme chemicals, the compound you speak of is much more of a challenge for you to obtain and absorb. Due to this, we recommend the ethically sourced supplementation available specifically to those following the plant-based diet. The holistic healers are available in abundance upon your planet to assist with that which you call 'nutritional deficiencies'. We might add that the receiving of plasmic light codes changes the configurations within, and this leaves the presentation of the laboratory readings to be useful as a guideline only. Your intuitions, when in absolute alignment, are always the wisest presentations to follow. The true pharmacy, physician and healer resides within.

I honestly think people should be able to eat whatever they want and not feel guilty if they eat meat. Don't you think you are making people feel guilty by suggesting they are going to get karma from eating meat?

It is correct that guilt can be triggered by many means and one way to trigger this within is to present that which resonates as deep and true aligned knowing within. Guilt is only felt by those who feel they are not following the true and aligned path they are called towards. Those who stand within knowing will not feel guilt regardless of what they consume or what anyone else presents to them regarding their dietary regime. These individuals are conscious and intuitive eaters and when they do this in balance, they feel only confidence, surety and knowing in their choices. Guilt itself is a signal, a message that something needs attention, re-evaluation and integration.

Is it not true that plants scream in agony when they are being killed or eaten? How can you say that they don't want to live any more than an animal or human does?

There is indeed a frequency change within the plant during the time of its transition. This is not what you would interpret as a 'scream' but it is a reaction. It is a mild resistance to the transition. There is not what you would term 'agony'. Different plants respond in different ways, yet all possess a will to live. We do not suggest that plants do not wish to live, they would not grow and flourish without the will to live. What we say here is that the resistance to the end of their existence is far less than that of the animal due to the fact that plants hold a collective consciousness and animals and humans hold individualised consciousness.

Do animals really have a soul? Surely their souls are not the same as a human soul? Would you not say they have 'awareness' rather than a soul?

Indeed, animals do have what you call a 'soul' which is an individualised matrix. This is a second dimensional matrix rather than a third dimensional matrix, but it is indeed what you call 'soul'. They have individualised awareness that is far more than simply an awareness of existing. The plant kingdom is that which holds awareness of existing. The animal holds the same awareness as the human but interprets that awareness through a second dimensional filter rather than third, which is instinctual. However, not all animals hold second dimensional matrices. For example, the dolphin holds a sixth dimensional matrix.

Some fruitarians only consume what falls to the ground naturally and will not pluck it from a tree. Are they therefore karma-free?

From the understanding within your fields in direct relation to your question the, aligned response would be yes. They would be karma-free from that point of view of the consuming of the naturally fallen fruits. However the overall karmic status will depend on their entire lifestyle and not just their diet.

I feel like I have been placed in a trap by God. I cannot ascend if I eat meat yet I get sick when I am vegan. Why the trap?

For an individual who is translating their reality this way, we would say to you that the way forward is through intuitive or conscious eating. Do all that you can to find the inner resonance, the inner voice, the inner teachers of light. When you stand within this inner knowing, there is no trap and all falls into place. There is no 'cannot' and there are no 'should nots'. There is simply following your alignment to light, your connection with the higher guidance system and the divine. One cannot go wrong or make mistakes when one follows the North Star that is their alignment, for even the mistake is part of the learning, growth and expansion. Your quest having found its way to us and the delivery of our response is part of this shift you are looking for. We wish you well in deciphering the conundrum presented as life's challenge and in the discovery of the gem within it.

I was told that in order to ground oneself then one should eat meat. Surely then, meat is useful if it is grounding?

This is indeed correct. The eating of the meat will work as a grounding tool for it anchors you to the third dimension, and the seafood to the fourth dimension. However, it is not grounding in the most beneficial way possible. Let us explain.

True grounding comes from anchoring the full pillar of light vertical axis from the root chakra below the feet earthing point into the crown chakra above the head cosmic point. The pillar remains balanced, vertical, strong, erect and unified. When eating meat, the root chakra (and to a certain extent, the sacral and the solar plexus chakra) is firmly rooted within the intensity of the anchoring. However, the higher points of the vertical axis are not aligned through this method. The reason for this is the meat has a binding effect rather than a rooting/anchoring/grounding in its true sense.

It is the difference between standing upon the rock for balance or being tied to the rock, unable to break free. The energetic is subtle and the ascending starseed can recoup the balance and reconstruct the temple through the vertical pillar after assimilation and detoxification. However, if one wishes to ground and anchor whilst retaining the vertical axis in its entirety, one would look to the large squashes or even more grounding/balancing would be the roots and the root vegetables. These can be obtained in many forms including the crushed, the powdered, the teas and the cooked whole foods. In certain cases, the raw root can be obtained.

The clue here is in the fact that the root is in and of itself 'a root' and is therefore utilised as 'rooting' (which is grounding into the Earth). Only balanced grounding can activate the full vertical axis pillar of light which is the foundation to the construction of the entire matrix.

Where does blood type come into this? Is it not true that some blood types are better vegan, whereas others need meat?

The blood type information is not without merit, however it is around twenty percent of the full picture. The true picture that follows along the same lines (individualised eating plan) is that of ancestry, and this includes soul ancestry as well as genetic lines. We speak here not only of that which you know as 'past lives' but also of soul matrix inception points such as Pleiadian, Sirian, Lyran or Arcturian. This is the reason, when looking at a template dietary plan for ascending starseeds (which is different to physical third dimensional non-ascending humans), that we present the Lemurian nutritional plan. The Lemurian civilisation includes souls from the Pleiades, Sirius and Lyra, amongst others.

What about when a lion kills a deer for food? Does that lion then get karma? Do animals get karma?

This we might say is an excellent question and shows growth within this subject area. The animals karmic path is 'different' but this is not to say they do not accumulate karma. Remember, karma is actually a cause and effect magnetic response. The animal in the case of your question, a lion, is very attuned towards its own cause and effect. The cause and effect is interwoven within the life plan or blueprint of the animal. Due to the fact that the lion's physiology needs to procure and consume the flesh of another animal, this is interwoven within the blueprint and life path of that animal. The lion is following its instinctual needs by killing and consuming the deer. This is indeed the 'circle of life' in action that is two dimensional (currently ascending into third dimensional). The instinctual consuming of another's life force in the way that the lion consumes the deer is showing you 'that which you are not' or rather 'that which you once were'. You can choose to still be this, and in the third dimension you still have the memory fields of the animal self.

When ascension (DNA reconstruction) begins to take place within the human, they move more towards the light, the compassion and the grace. This includes creating as little suffering as possible. Therefore, one can honour the lion and the circle of life knowing that one has moved beyond that dimensional expression, if one makes the choice to do so. As we have said, there is no judgement regarding your choices.

So whilst the lion will reap karma (as that is inevitable when incarnated within physicality), it will be in direct proportion to the physiological needs of that being (animal or human). The lion will cease to live if it does not eat the flesh of other animals and it would be against the lion's blueprinted destiny not to kill and eat the deer. Therefore, karma is not the same. It does not present as an opportunity for a lesson or for integration. It reinforces the lion's cosmic blueprint as a soul for it is doing what it must do and what it is designed to do. The experience of consuming the other animal's flesh and life force is its destiny.

From this perspective we could say that when the lion kills and consumes the deer, it is living more in alignment than most of the incarnated humans do! This is because the lion is so instinctual that it rarely, if ever, leaves the blueprinted path. There is less scope for movement away from the path but because of this, there is less availability for expansion. The human has far more choices to make and has a far wider terrain in which to move within and away from the blueprinted path, and thus is given a far greater chance for expansion. This is simply the difference between second density experience and third density experience.

From this perspective (that of the lion living it's destiny), we could say that the lion is 'karma-free'. Although it is actually not the case, for the lion will eventually (on a soul level) learn the lesson regarding keeping oneself alive through consuming and suffering of others. On a soul level, it will eventually learn how to keep oneself nourished and alive by choosing the path that involves the least suffering possible. The lion must ascend the second density into the third density and become human in order to learn this lesson, or be presented with this experience. All the experiences are placed within the blueprint prior to incarnation.

However, the 'blueprint' goes with you (into your incarnation). It is that which we call the 'matrix' and it can be changed from the incarnational path within the third dimension. The ability to change the matrix is fourth and fifth dimensional. This is presented to you in our transmission *Masters of the Matrix*.[1]

You speak of souls inception points. Is an individual more likely to crave meat if their inception point is Sirian, Lyran or Pleiadian? Are these inception points related to blood groups?

Blood groups come into it but, as we said, are only a small part of the picture. Once chooses one's blood group when choosing an incarnation but this is alongside conducive astrological alignments, genetic traits and abilities, location and the potential for aligned experience. Therefore we cannot say that one blood group is Sirian and the other Lyran. We may also mention that despite the inception point, which is only a linear interpretation, the majority of starseeds have had incarnations upon, or are connected to, all three planetary systems (and many other systems, these three are the most usual as a linear inception point).

However, if we had to break this down we could say that Pleiadian and Lyran individuals are more likely to gravitate towards the plant-based eating and the Sirian soul is more likely to eat meat. Lyran souls have a great affinity for birds and the avian races. Those with Lyran inception points are extremely repelled by the idea of eating poultry or eggs of any kind as they see this as their family. Sirian individuals hold a higher trait for the predatory so do crave the animal flesh. However, all ascending starseeds have other aspects within them, that of cosmic light and the memory of being beyond the individualised planetary experience.

This is why we encourage you to follow the conscious or intuitive eating, for this is the way to access the divine blueprint. The starseed diet will always be predominantly plant-based even if animal flesh is consumed in small amounts. The reason for this is because the raw plant materials are the conductors of light and

---

1   "Masters of the Matrix" (2016) by Magenta Pixie

they hold the codes and messages within, that are needed to fuse or merge with the DNA of the ascending individual.

What about wearing clothing made of animals or sitting on a leather sofa? If most of our products are animal-based, is this unavoidable karma?

The karma is most minimal if sitting upon furnitures that are not your own and that are simply in the greater society. The karma is more significant when the clothing or household goods are purchased by the individual, however even these are minimal next to the consuming of the factory farmed animal flesh. Consuming something, taking it within your physical body so that all its cells and chemical instructions become part of you, is very different to the wearing of the clothing or the utilising of the household items. The karma is minimal.

However, we might add that there is a growing karmic load accumulated regarding some of your clothings and technologies due to suffering caused by those who are forced to undertake the work involved in the creation of these items. If you can trace back the supply chain of your goods and discover corruption and suffering, then indeed there will be a karmic response to the purchasing and owning of that item. When the individual is aware of the suffering or exploitation within the supply chain, the karma accumulated is greater than the individual who is unaware. However, ignorance holds its own karmic pattern that is released through accumulation of knowledge and awareness.

The way forward for the starseed is to do whatever they can to reduce suffering, for they remain within a service-to-others positive polarised frequency when they do this and this is the frequency they need for their ascension process.

The distraction created by worry or alarm that one is creating suffering and thus karma with every purchase is also not in the highest good of the ascending one. Therefore, we say again, follow the intuitions, the gut feelings, the inner teachers and the higher guidance. Your alignment will always direct you to the highest path or the most aligned choice for you in that moment.

For example, you may need to choose between needing a transportation device such as a vehicle, yet know that suffering was potentially caused in its supply chain. Or the item may be a medical necessity or a communication device. One would look for the item that holds the highest vibration, taking into account the supply chain and the appropriateness of the item in relation to that which it is needed for. Simply being conscientious and aware, and taking steps towards compassion and away from suffering, moves you into a positively polarised cause and effect field (meaning that you receive 'good karma' if you will - as we have said, there is no 'good' or 'bad' here but we use this term for ease of explanation).

What about children being given meat as part of their diet? Do they get karma for eating it?

The child does not accumulate karma in the same way as the adult. The karma accumulated is in direct alignment with the awareness of the individual. There is much 'cosmic leeway' or 'allowance' made for the child when it comes to their growth, learning and balance.

Shouldn't children be given animal products as they are still growing?

We have mentioned that there are two aspects to nutritional need. One is cleansing and the other is nourishing. It is the nourishing diet that one would be looking towards for the growing child. Whilst this can be found in a carefully planned plant-based diet, we would say that the natural, unspoiled and sustainably raised animal products are in alignment for the physiological needs of most children. There are starseed children with high awareness and soul memory who will reject the animal product however, and a wise parent will follow this if it is coming from genuine intuition and knowing on behalf of the child. The raw goats milk is most in alignment for the growing child, the milk from the cow does not align with human physiology. If the child rejects the milk from the goat then the other milk, most in alignment with the majority of starseeds (both children and adult), would be the milk from the coconut.

Are you saying that if I eat meat then I will not gain entry into the fifth dimensional Gaia?

This is not what is being said here. Your entry into fifth dimensional Gaia will depend on many things. However, regular consuming of factory farmed animals who have suffered, with their meat holding the pain/death vibration, will accumulate karma (and toxicity) above the level needed for ascension. Therefore we can say it will be a rare individual indeed who 'gains entry' into Gaia with a continuous bellyful of pain-infused animal flesh.

Will my physiology change to the point where I no longer need to eat food at all?

The answer to this is yes. However, this may not be in the current lifetime you experience. This physiological change to the point where one 'lives on light' may occur 'several incarnations' in your future. However, your current now moment (2019 at the time of this transmission) is where your planet undergoes collective ascension. However, there are stages to that ascension process. Many starseeds are living their 'last life' if you will. This simply means that they no longer need to incarnate within a third dimensional physical existence 'after' their current life. The most predominant eating style for the collective of the ascending ones is that of a plant-based diet, mimicking the Lemurian diet that we have presented. There will be some individuals within this ascension process that move to the living on light through physiological change within their current life. More and more starseeds are drawn to this way of living and intrinsically know this is their calling. Many will at first be drawn to periods of fasting or following a liquid diet only. The yearning for a higher and higher vibration within the diet will accompany ascension. Ultimately the ascending individuals physiology is moving in this direction and will eventually be such that food, in the form you are accustomed to in third density, will no longer be needed to sustain your vehicle.

Is it not true that plants produce anti-nutrients?

It depends what you mean by 'anti-nutrients'. This would suggest that they produce that which is against nutrition. The truth is that plants are abundant in nutrition. However, plants do produce difficult to digest compounds. Some of these compounds are perfect for human physiology and some are not. So some of these could be called anti-nutrients in the case of a human diet. These would be the plants that cause the body to lose nutrition. However, as we have said, there is no one perfect diet for all humans. These anti-nutrients may cause one human to lose nutrition or create digestive issue, and yet the same plant may give nutrition and create healing for another human. Your question therefore cannot be replied to as a 'yes' or 'no' answer, although ultimately the response would be a 'yes', they do naturally produce these.

Is this not their way of protecting themselves from being eaten?

It is their way of protecting themselves from being eaten by the species that would not benefit from eating them. In nature (in a naturally flowing, harmonious and aligned third dimensional planet), the plants that grow are part of an ecosystem. They hold codes, light, information and other properties that other species living close by to that plant need. There is a reciprocal energetic between the plant that grows and the being that will sustain themselves from consuming that plant. Therefore, the protecting of themselves is as much a signal to the being that would not benefit from their consumption as it is a means of protection. It ensures they are consumed only when the benefit is reciprocal to that particular plant collective consciousness as well as the being doing the consuming. We realise that your planet is not naturally flowing, harmonious and aligned due to the hijacking that has taken place. However, one can find the harmony if one knows how to work with harmonious flow within themselves.

Does this not then prove that their will to live is strong?

It proves that nature, when left alone to flourish, has the innate intelligence to sustain the species that exist upon that planet. It is not necessarily the 'will to live' that is strong in the plant but the 'will to reproduce as a plant species' that is strong. The anti-nutrients do not necessarily ensure life but they do ensure reproduction. If the species that will benefit from consuming that plant eats it, then through the physiological digestion and elimination system, the being will give that plant species the chance at reproducing.

Should humans therefore be eliminating outdoors and not in bathrooms?

The natural way is the harmonious and aligned way. If a being is eating only a species specific diet, then the elimination substance will be valuable. However, humanity on your planet does not follow the species specific diet as a general rule. Therefore the elimination substance produced will be toxic to the environment and not beneficial enough to be recycled.

Are the anti-nutrients 'lectins' and 'phytates' harmful for human consumption?

That which you call 'lectins' and 'phytates' are many and varied and it is far beyond the scope of this transmission to present to you that information. What we can say is some of these are harmful to some humans and others are beneficial. This is why we encourage you to follow the conscious and intuitive eating plan.

I have done all I can to remain vegan but I simply cannot live healthily without eating animal products. What does this mean for me? Has my good karma run out?

One's 'good karma' does not run out. There is cause and effect in all things. Every positive thought or action you emanate as the result of aligned positive intention will reap the aligned match.

If the plant-based diet is not in alignment for you and your physiology at this time and the eating of animal products is bringing your physiology into balance, then this is the way forward for you. We would say again that the starseed is advised to source the sustainably and ethically raised animal products rather than the factory farmed.

Is it true that in the wild there is a contract between the hunter and the hunted?

This is correct from the higher dimensional perspective. This is incorrect from a third dimensional perspective. Once the animal has incarnated into physicality, the will to live within its pre-incarnate blueprint is activated through the animal's free will. The contract remains in place in the higher dimensional realities and is that which we call 'destiny'. There is no contract in the third dimension and that is what we call 'free will'. They run alongside one another.

When the animal realises it is in a contract with the hunter, it then gives itself to the hunter and allows itself to be killed. Is this correct?

The animal does not realise from the third dimensional perspective that it is in a contract with the hunter. The animal may know this on a deep intrinsic level but the will to live and the resistance to death is far greater than the contract in that moment.

This is akin to saying that the man with the gun and the victim are in a contract. When the victim realises he is in a contract with the gunman, he allows himself to be shot. It is the same thing.

Are the hunter and the hunted not part of the circle of life? So surely it is normal and natural?

The circle of life you speak of, in this context, is betwixt predatory animal and other animal. Once the human began to make tools with which to hunt, then they removed themselves from the natural circle of life. The only animal that would be considered part of the circle of life with the human would be the animal that the human caught with his bare hands.

Were they not supposed to create tools though? Is this not human evolution?

Indeed. With human evolution comes new responsibility and new paradigms. We are not saying it is a negative act to utilise tools to catch one's food, we are simply saying that one can no longer class the use of the tool as part of the circle of life.

Is it not as simple as doing what feels right and good for you?

If this feeling of doing what feels right and good for you comes from genuine intuition and inner guidance then yes, it is as simple as that. However, many individuals do not have access to true intuition. Therefore, triggers and keycodes are provided through various means, and the meaningful subjective experience of that individual, so that they may access that innate wisdom or intuition.

If the feeling of what is right and good for you comes from simply wanting to do whatever you please and this causes suffering to another being, then no, it is not as simple as this.

I mean, if there is no right or wrong or good or bad, how are we getting caught up on this?

When it comes to karma, there is no right or wrong or good or bad in the sense that karma simply is as it is, a universal law of cause and effect without judgement. However, this cannot be taken literally within the linear physical experience. If it is taken literally then an individual can decide to make a choice that causes harm to others without consequence. Therefore, indeed there is right and wrong (or positive and negative action) within the linear physical reality which is a polarised and dualistic existence. Only within the higher realms is there no polarity, no duality and only oneness. From that point of view there is no right or wrong, good or bad, positive or negative for all is one and unified. One must integrate the unification with the compartmentalised polarity within the third dimension. If one does not do this, they apply higher dimensional laws to the physical universe. When they do this, they are lost to all reason and sanity (that which we call 'ungrounded').

Just eat what you want. What is the problem and why is it anyone else's business?

What you eat should not be the business of another, you are quite correct. Yet when suffering of other beings occurs on such a grand scale as it does on your planet, there will be those who take up the torch to fight for the rights of those suffering animals. They stand as guardians to the beings, in this case the animals who are seen by these human guardians as 'not having a voice'. By the action of taking up the torch and becoming the guardian for that animal, they then take the perspective that the suffering the animals endure through mass farming for human consumption is indeed 'a problem'. This, from their perspective, is seen as their business.

We are not saying their perspective is either correct or incorrect within the greater reality. What we are saying is that their perspective is correct for them just as your perspective is correct for you.

Is it not the case that vegans cannot understand why meat eaters eat meat and that they are some of the most judgemental individuals on the planet?

This is indeed the case for some individuals following the vegan path. They can become so entrenched within their belief system and hold such anger (justified, we might add, from the perspective they hold) at the treatment of the factory farmed animals that they do hold judgement and they do hold a paradigm of confusion regarding anyone who consumes those animals.

Some vegans take this further and hold the viewpoint that all animals, including sustainably raised animals, should not simply be raised for food. These individuals do hold a valid perspective. Whilst sustainably raised meat holds less 'karma' in its consumption because the suffering is less (and in many cases there is no suffering at all), it is still not part of the natural circle of life to raise an animal, keep that animal in captivity (however well treated) and then cull that animal for food. These vegans do not believe in eating animals in any form. Their deeply held beliefs can lead to confusion, anger and judgement.

However, there are a great many vegans who do not allow their opinions and belief systems to be the cause of anger or judgement towards another. Your question therefore cannot be responded to in its entirety for the way you phrase your question places 'vegans' as a unit, all in the same category. The question rephrased to 'some vegans' or even 'many vegans' is far more in alignment. It cannot apply to 'all vegans'.

When vegans behave that way then it puts me off ever considering giving up meat. So if their aim is to convert me, it is actually doing the opposite.

We can fully understand your thought process here. Control, pushing and force is not the way to achieve a goal. There must be surrender, acceptance and freedom in all cases.

I understand karma from past life memory.

This is one way that the law of karma can be understood. Memory itself, 'past life' or 'future life' or 'alternate life' is the way to enlightenment.

You say it is an energetic match like the law of attraction, but I see it simply as coming from self.

Indeed. There is only self. The self is at one with the environment. The environment is simply externalised perception of self. The energetic match that is law of attraction is part of that perceived externalised self, therefore it is self. Your statement is therefore correct.

No one makes the decisions but me because there is nothing outside of me.

This is correct within the higher dimensions. However, in third density, due to duality and free will of another, one cannot make decisions that impact the natural evolution and expansion of another without consequence.

Therefore I can do what I want and I don't need to worry about karma which will interfere with my enjoyment of life.

Indeed, this is true unless the 'doing what you want' impacts the evolution and expansion of another. If the 'doing what you want' does not impact the evolution and expansion of another (this would include place, community, thought construct, creation and intention of another also) then you would not need to 'worry' about karma as you would be in the state we may call 'karma-free'.

The only way to achieve the 'doing what you want' without impacting upon the reality of another is to fully follow the incarnational blueprint that you created for yourself before you were born into physicality. However, that incarnational blueprint will include the learning and expansion through the 'making the mistakes' if you will. Therefore it is a very rare individual who can live their entire lives doing whatever they want without impacting upon the reality of another.

If I decide I have made a mistake but then forgive myself, then that lesson is learned. Karma is therefore my business and no one else's.

This is indeed correct. However, not all incarnated individuals are able to truly decide if they have 'made a mistake'. There are many who consider their actions to be neutral, positive and beneficial without realising that they are impacting upon the reality of another (and thus the other's evolution and expansion).

The forgiveness of self is an important, significant and extremely beneficial tool and it is wise that you mention this. It is true that if you are following the aligned blueprinted path, karma is therefore 'your business'. However, as we have said, if your action impacts upon another being (and in the case of this discussion, we are speaking of animals who have suffered greatly to become food) then 'karma' is not simply your business from the third dimensional perspective due to the fact that 'karma' is a consequence of your decision or action. This may impact another which makes it 'their' business (or that of their self-appointed guardian).

Karma is therefore the greatest teaching tool you have within your third dimensional reality. Or again, we could refer to karma as 'cause and effect' or the 'law of magnetic attraction'.

Have the service-to-self groups not impacted upon the rest of humanity's evolution and expansion, and thus their free will?

Indeed. Hence the reason we bring to you our transmissions in order to assist and guide you into 'rising up' if you will, and reclaiming your power and independence so you may continue to evolve, expand and access your divine right to free will.

What about the fact that I feed my dog and my cat meat? Do they get karma?

This is most similar to the quest regarding the lion and the deer. Karma works differently within the second dimension. The physiology of all felines need meat in order to survive and it is species specific for most canines even though they can exist without it. Due to the fact that the eating of meat is part of their destiny, karma would not be accumulated in the same way. Within second density, everything is instinctual and instant in that regard. However, regarding cats and dogs specifically, they live close to humans and they are therefore closer to the third dimension. The cat or the dog eating the man-made foodstuffs from the packets and the jars is not the same as the circle of life that is the lion and the deer. Therefore the cat and the dog become somewhat connected to the karmic pathway of the human family they exist with. The dog especially is a pack animal and, whilst an individualised soul, would also reap the karma 'cause and effect' of the entire pack. Therefore one could say that the karma for the domesticated animals is somewhat more impactful towards their overall growth as a soul than the animal living in the wild. Yet the human's karma is intertwined very closely with that of the pet they care for.

Are you saying humans get karma just for owning a pet?

Remembering that one does not 'get' karma, it is an energetic flowing through you, of which you are part. But yes, on a collective level the domestication of all animals, taking them from their natural habitat and creating specific breed types for humans pleasure and enjoyment, does create a collective karma. This can be neutralised through the loving and close connections you have with your pets, many of which are soul connections between pet and owner. We are not saying for you to not adopt pets, for the love and healing shared with your pets is of an extremely high vibration. Having a feline live within your household raises the vibrational frequency of the entire house. We are simply saying that there is collective karma from the historical domestication in the first place.

So there is individual karma (based on your thoughts, words, actions and deeds) and collective karma (based on humanity's thoughts, words, actions and deeds).

So when Jesus died on the cross and it is said that he 'died for our sins', is this meaning that he took on the karma of humanity and cleared it?

This is a long and complex subject and beyond the scope of this transmission. Let us just say that the symbolic presentation here is that individuals who ascend to higher consciousness are able to 'clear karma for others' as they influence humanity's collective consciousness the most.

I am of the understanding that whatever you eat carries no karma if you bless it and are grateful.

This understanding is correct if that which you consume is in alignment with the frequency you create through your blessing. This would not include toxic foods or animal flesh containing fear/death codes. No amount of blessing from one individual can transmute foodstuffs that are toxic to the body or neutralise the lifetime suffering of an animal.

A large group of empowered and activated individuals however can make an impact upon these things. The blessing must be equal in intensity to that which is being blessed.

Therefore if you bless the animal flesh upon your plate, this makes no difference to the karmic energy you accrue if that animal has suffered and you consume it. The blessing will assist you in feeling better and removing guilt, which is most positive, but it will not change the karma you receive or the energetic match you create.

Surely once I die and cross over to the other side, then I will learn the truth of all this?

This will depend on the energetic you hold within your overall body mind system and the 'coordinates' in place regarding the 'place' you go when you 'cross over to the other side'.

Why do I need to learn this now?

There is no difference between learning, growth or expansion within your physical incarnation or after it. One is done within the body, the other is done as a non-physical individualised matrix without the body. The vibrational frequency of the learning is the same.

Isn't it better to just live my life and learn my lessons when I cross over?

It is one option. It is not necessarily 'better' but it is the most usual way for the incarnated human. The aware starseed will understand that the now is the now. There is no 'waiting to cross over' as everything is experienced from the current moment. That is ascension and one does not have to leave the physical body to ascend.

Is it not true that we need fat in our diets and we can only get the right fat from animals?

It is not true that every human being needs added or extra fats to their diets (even plants contain fat). Yet there are humans incarnated upon your planet who can survive and thrive without fat, just as there are humans who can survive without solid food at all.

The majority of humans however would need some form of fat within their diets. This does not have to be from an animal source. Many individuals can access all the fats they need to survive and thrive from plant-based sources. Other individuals do find that they need animal fats. As we have said, there is no one blanket diet that is correct for every human being. For the ascending starseed, the Lemurian diet is the closest plan to that which is most in alignment on a general level.

Fat soluble vitamins do not absorb in our bodies on a vegan diet.

It is correct that these compounds you speak of are not fully absorbed by some individuals eating fully plant-based. It is correct that conversion of these compounds into the useable state is not optimal by some individuals. However, there are other individuals who are able to absorb and convert these compounds on a fully plant-based diet. Hence the reason that we encourage you to follow your intuition and your guidance, making sure that which you know and feel is truly coming from the guidance within. This is not just an intrinsic knowing but also presents itself through synchronicity. For example, an individual asking and praying to be shown the healing path and then they find the exact book they need, detailing exactly what they need to consume in order to heal.

Conscious eating is the paramount, predominant and priority way forward in this regard.

Is it not true that Jesus drank alcohol and ate fish? How then is all this true, for surely Jesus is the greatest master ever to walk the planet?

This would entail a long and complex response in order to present accurate truth which is outside the scope of this transmission. There was more than one individual whose life became the basis for the individual you know as 'Jesus' within your Bible.

Therefore it is not fully possible to respond in any truly meaningful way here, except to say that the 'Jesus' you know was an Essene. He grew up and lived with the Essenes and ate a fully one hundred percent raw plant-based diet.

However, the other individuals who collectively make up 'Jesus' would have eaten a little fish and other seafood and drank the wine. However, the fish would have been from clean unpolluted waters and the wine would be naturally fermented and of a very high quality.

Regarding Jesus being 'the greatest master ever to walk the planet', all we can say here is that 'he who holds Christ consciousness is the greatest master to ever walk the planet'. This would be far closer to the truth.

We would also say, regarding your Bible, rather than you seeing your Biblical stories as historical, it would assist you to utilise them more efficiently by seeing them as your future.

I think saying that you can get karma by eating meat leads to elitism. The vegans will then somehow think they are more evolved than everyone else.

This indeed can be the case. However, elitism is that which we would refer to as the 'god complex'. Anyone acting from this way of thinking would not be in alignment with the ascension timeline or with the frequencies created by consuming a naturally high vibrational plant-based diet. It is unlikely that the high frequency created by this way of eating would create god complex mentality. It is more in alignment with compassion and surrender which is the opposite, that of humility. Therefore presenting truth regarding karmic balance and the consuming of animal flesh and their products is unlikely to lead to elitism on a large scale.

We would also add that the fully conscious plant-based eater of natural whole plants, also taking the spiritual path in life and thus ascension, is 'more evolved' than the other individuals upon the planet. From the perspective of evolution itself. The reason being is that their DNA configuration is more encoded with plasmic light and further into crystalline than carbon. Crystalline is further along the evolutionary path than carbon. However, just because these particular spiritually aware plant-based eaters (and this does not mean all vegans) are 'more evolved than', it does not mean they are 'better than'. From that perspective, all are equal and none are more aware of this fact than the ascending individuals we speak of.

I get spaced-out if I live on a vegan diet for too long and then I have to eat meat to ground myself. Am I getting karma for this? Would it be better to just stay spaced-out even though I feel weird?

This depends what you mean by 'spaced-out'. There is a certain 'lightness' that occurs with plant-based eaters (hence the higher vibration) and some cannot ground this frequency into the physical body. We have discussed the grounding versus binding effect of meat so we would draw your attention towards the roots for this purpose. The awakened individual needs the 'spaced-out' feeling that you speak of for this is Kundalini activation and pineal gland activation. These are needed for higher connection and visionary work. Our conduit is 'spaced-out' as she types our words. However if she were to eat meat, she would lose the ability to make such a clear connection with us. There are many ways to ground oneself without eating animal flesh, however. If you find you do not need this Kundalini frequency, or if it is too much for you at this time, and the only way you can truly move away from it and feel better in yourself is to eat meat, then we would say do this. As we have said, this is about conscious and intuitive eating. The karma, as we have said, is minimal when the individual lives within positive polarisation in all other aspects of their lives and the animal flesh or product being consumed was sustainably and ethically raised. However, indeed you would take on the karma of creating suffering to another if you were to consume factory farmed meat. The death/pain vibration codes would enter your body, become part of you and create the matching energetic within your reality.

It would not be 'better' to stay spaced-out if you are not utilising the Kundalini awakening. The starseeds are going through these Kundalini awakenings en masse during your current time period as part of the ascension process and indeed, it does take time to learn to adjust to these frequencies.

Can dogs or cats live a vegan life and be healthy?

A feline cannot survive without meat. A canine can survive without meat and some may live in a healthy state. However, the vegan diet would not be optimum for the canine. The optimum diet for the canine would be meat-based.

I don't eat meat myself but I do buy it and cook it for my family. Am I getting the karma just for purchasing and cooking?

The karma here would be very similar to the sitting on the furnitures or wearing the clothing or owning the technologies. To purchase the factory farmed meat is not an 'ethical purchase' so indeed there would be karma. However, this is not the same as actually consuming the animal and taking it into your body. If you own a cat or a dog, you would be purchasing and preparing meat for that animal. Karma would be neutral here for the caring of the animal would balance the purchase of the meat. Karma is simply balance. The energetic of balance within your reality.

Preparing and cooking meat for your family is, in a karmic sense, similar to preparing meat for the cat or the dog. The only difference is that the cat or dog needs the meat to survive. The human family may or may not need animal products. If you are preparing ethically raised and nourishing animal foods for your child, karma is negligible. One can feel the balance if one tunes into the intrinsic knowing within. Or one can give the quest to the higher aspect of self and the aligned response shall come.

I am plant-based except for that I drink bone broth. It is meant to be so healthy for you. Is this true? Am I getting karma just by drinking bone broth?

The drinking of the bone broth would fall into the 'nourishing foods' category. However, so too would the drinking of the vegetable broth. Drinking the broth made from the boiling of the animal bones is no different karmically than eating the flesh. If that animal has suffered and was factory farmed then the death/ pain frequency is there and it can often be concentrated in the bone even more than the flesh. The karma is the same. However, if the rest of your diet is fully plant-based, then karma is lessened if that is the only animal product you consume. To lessen karma even more, make sure the animal bones are from an ethically raised animal.

I was under the impression that you need to be fifty-one percent service-to-others and then you can ascend.

Your overall vibration needs to be higher in the service-to-others frequency than the service-to-self. Fifty-one percent would take you into ascension but not full stargate ascension. Meaning that you would 'ride on the coat-tails' of the fully ascending being, or a more appropriate metaphor would be that you would 'ride on the back of the dragon' but you would not be the dragon rider who steers the dragon. However, this matters not. Ascension is ascension and yes, you would ascend at fifty-one percent service-to-others.

So surely I can eat meat, but if my actions in life are compassionate and loving then I will automatically become at least fifty-one percent service-to-others and will ascend. How then is eating meat preventing my ascension?

You are correct. Eating sustainably raised meat would not prevent your ascension in this case. However, regarding factory farmed animals, the suffering they endure is just too great to take you to fifty-one percent service-to-others. The mass torture and sacrifice of these animals is a fully service-to-self act and consuming the flesh will take you into the service-to-self vibration. This would prevent your ascension. The only way ascension could be achieved would be if the amount of factory farmed flesh you consumed was extremely infrequent and minimal. One cannot always generalise and there are exceptions to the rule. The factory farmed animals have placed out a call collectively for the end of their suffering. They continue to go through this suffering within a trapped reincarnational cycle in order to teach compassion to the world. Part of the starseed's mission is to answer their call and end their suffering. This is one of the reasons so many starseeds are drawn to the vegan path. If you continue to consume their flesh, you are not answering their call. As we have said, it is a rare person indeed who can consume the flesh of another who has suffered and still ascend.

The only other exception to this rule would be if that particular human is completely isolated from accessing sustainably raised meat and must eat animal flesh in order to survive. In this case, ascension may be possible if that individual's true desire and intention were to cease eating factory farmed meat and to source the sustainably raised but they were unable to do so. This case would be most rare but a potential.

If we are all one, are we not just eating ourselves when we eat meat? The circle of life?

From the higher perspective, yes this is correct.

If so, how is this in any way a bad thing?

It is not a 'bad thing', as we have said. Karma is not a judgement. However when you exist within the third dimension, in physical form, experiencing a linear reality, you are not 'at one' with the animal. You are separate, individual beings and one is able to cause harm and suffering to the other. That action has a reaction. It is the law of the universe. This is what you call 'karma'.

You categorise and compartmentalise and put things into order and sequence, but is this not directly contradictory to unification and oneness?

Yes. It is directly contradictory from the third dimensional perspective. However, we are looking here at laws and perspectives in different dimensions which are indeed perceived as contradictory. Within the third dimension, one needs to categorise and compartmentalise in order to sort, analyse and place in order. Within the higher dimensions, there is unification and oneness. Compartmentalisation does not exist there. Within one's ascension journey, one learns to live by the laws within each dimension whilst holding the memory structure of the other. This is the only route to stargate ascension, for one cannot construct the divine architecture of self without this understanding. This is what we refer to as 'bilocational, triliocational and multilocational consciousness into omnipresence'. This is explained in detail in our previous transmission *The Infinite Helix and the Emerald Flame.*[2]

Rodents, birds and insects die to produce a field of grain. How is this not karma? How is this any worse than eating meat?

Indeed, there would be karma on the disruption of the wildlife's habitat. This is not at the same level as actually consuming animal flesh, however some animals have been through extreme suffering when losing their habitat in this way. The higher karma lands upon the farmer and, in a lesser sense, the one who consumes the grain. As we have said before, consuming plants is not without karma. There is no 'better' or 'worse' here. As we have said, this is simply about the balancing of one's reality.

What about the conversion of ALA to EPA and DHA. I was under the impression that this cannot be done efficiently when eating only plants, therefore some fish must surely be required?

It is correct that there are many plant-based eaters unable to convert from one codex to the more useable form, as you say. The algae oils which are already converted can be of assistance here, but it is true that in some cases the fish needs to be consumed. Seafood binds you to the fourth dimension, not the third as they exist within the ocean which is very akin to etheric, fourth dimensional plasma. Therefore one is not as 'bound' and karma is less than the eating of the land animal as the fish does not resist its death as much as the land animal. However, the resistance is still there.

There are plant-based eaters that are able to convert the codex to the more useable form quite successfully. In fact, after a period of

2   "The Infinite Helix and the Emerald Flame" (2018) by Magenta Pixie

time, the body becomes aware that the precursor form is the only form being consumed so begins to convert more and more. This conversion is lost when the useable form is then consumed. So in some plant-based eaters, consuming fish or their oils is actually detrimental to that conversion process. Many variables here. Again we say that the intuitive and the conscious eating is the path to follow.

Some of the most spiritual people I have ever met have been meat eaters, and some of the most pretentious and least spiritual have been vegans. I therefore cannot conclude that being vegan is the way to go.

The premise must be a balanced one in order to come to an aligned conclusion. It is quite correct that many deeply spiritual individuals are meat eaters and that some individuals with no spiritual energy or understanding are plant-based. However, the reverse equation is also true. As we have said, many variables. Therefore your conclusion is based upon a premise only you have experienced which is not a true and accurate depiction of reality.

One's diet is not a reflection of a person's spiritual awareness and awakenedness.

This is true in the sense that many spiritual individuals, moving into mastery, have eaten animal flesh. However, what has been historical upon your planet is not necessarily the continued status quo. Your peoples are undergoing an ascension process along with the planet. 'Being spiritual' and 'going through ascension', though extremely connected, are in fact two different things. We speak here within this question and response transmission predominantly to those undergoing ascension and specifically stargate ascension.

Karma is not taken on like a future burden.

Indeed it is not. It is simply balance.

You live the entire life of the animal in parallel to your own.

This is correct only from the perspective whereby you live every being's life that has ever existed (for you are unified). However, in a literal sense and on a linear level it is not the case that you live the entire life of the animal you consume. This is a metaphor to explain the law of karma.

I used to enjoy eating meat, sugar and drinking wine. Yet now I feel pain in my body when I eat meat and I feel sick when eating sugar and drinking wine. Why is this happening?

The meat, sugar and wine are no longer aligning with your vibrational field. You are no longer a vibrational match to these things. As you raise in frequency, everything that is no longer a vibrational match to you will leave your reality and this includes food.

The height of human arrogance is to think we have any control over the actual manifestations and the outcomes of our accumulated karma.

We can understand your perspective. For the law of karma is most sacred. The actual manifestations of karma are not controlled or influenced by anything other than the law of karma itself, which is a living and intelligent frequency. A being, if you will. He is known as 'the Lord of Karma' and has many names.

However, you can step into the awareness of that karma accumulation and discover some sense of the energetic output and its equal and opposite reaction that is cause and effect. The sensitive, empathic, aware individual can communicate with 'the Lord of Karma' if you will, and find ways to walk as a being within third dimensional reality as a 'karma-free soul'.

It takes more than one lifetime to do this.

Indeed, this is correct. However, a great many individuals - we call them 'starseeds' - have lived these lifetimes and are now accomplishing the challenging task of consciously balancing their karma. This is all part of the ascension process and we are 'most pleased' to see how well the starseeds are doing in this regard.

7: The Fall and the Climb

You spoke of the Lemurian people beginning to eat the fruits as they became more third dimensional. Can you explain this process and did they start eating meat?

This process took many of your Earth years, if you will, if you measure this in linear time. The time was experienced differently in early Lemurian times as this was very much a zero-point energy field. This which you know as 'the fall' took place over millennia.

The DNA sequencing simply responded to the environment (although it is true to say that the environment responds to the DNA sequencing within the life forms that exist within the environment).

The rise and fall of the energy frequencies and light quotients within the human vehicle is a natural and organic process, just as is breathing. The pattern follows, if you will, the sine wave. However, this process was 'hijacked'. Yet this is only truth within the fourth and third dimensions (depending on reality model used). Within the fifth dimensions and above, the 'hijacking' was a choice made in order to create free will amongst the falling humans.

At this time there was another civilisation beginning on your Earth, those that you know as 'Atlanteans'.

The Lemurians were predominantly full plant eaters, although later Lemurians began to eat small fish and other sea life. Some drank milk from the animal (closely resembling your goat of your now), although predominantly the milk they drank was from the coconut.

The Lemurians were large in stature. You would see them as giants. Yet as they fell in consciousness, they fell also in size becoming more and more like your peoples of your modern-day.

They were connected to the higher consciousness and were aware of themselves as unified beings and representations of pure Source energy. As they fell, they began to forget (or rather they simply lost) the knowing of this connection. It was around this time that the Atlantean civilisation began upon your planet and it was at this time that animals began to be seen as food.

A few Lemurians began to eat the flesh of small animals but the majority of Lemurians remained fully plant eaters.

The Atlanteans were the ones who began to eat meat, although even in this society there were fully plant-based eaters.

The diet that the individual consumed was in direct relation to the light quotient within their overall matrix, the DNA activation and the environment.

The Lemurians were a peaceful people, with little conflict. Yet the Lemurians did not operate fully within a free will, choice-based reality.

The decision to bring in free will and choice amongst these humans was in order to present them with growth and expansion. The Lemurians were a beautiful people, existing in harmony, yet growth and expansion was slower.

The plan was to bring the peoples of Earth back to the point of the Lemurian knowing of the connectedness with Source, whilst at the same time allowing them the free will and choice to experience multiple emotions and to discover themselves through a myriad of circumstances and situations. Thus could Source so too know itself.

You are right now, in your now reality, at the point where you have been through the myriad of opportunity, circumstance and situation and you return to the oneness and the harmony and the beauty of the Lemurian races with the knowledge and experience of the fully physical vehicle. In order for you to get where you are now, you had to experience the separation and the forgetting.

The starseeds on Earth today are the result of this choice, made millennia ago upon your planet within linear time.

The original Lemurians before the fall, and in the early stages of the fall, did not experience linear time. You, dear starseeds of the now time (the 2012 time period of the great awakening), are now moving back to this same experience where you do not experience linear time. You are currently experiencing non-linear and linear time simultaneously as you begin the climb.

When the Lemurians fell and the Atlantean civilisation began (there was an overlap between the ending of the Lemurian age and the beginning of the Atlantean age, but this took thousands upon thousands of your Earth years), the meat eating was 'necessary' if you will. The reason for this was that the newly third dimensional physical body could not sustain in its full optimum health without the meat.

The trees bearing ripe delicious fruits, abundant with full amino acid profiles within, began to grow less and less. This was due to the fall in environment. You see, as the physical third dimension was created it was not just the individuals that fell in frequency but the planet also. Or rather, should we say the 'sphere' you existed upon. It was not a physical 'planet' at that time but a higher dimensional version of one. You see, the individuals inhabiting the sphere create the density of the sphere itself. They do this through thought structure, yet this is a whole other topic and outside the scope of this particular transmission.

When the light bodies of the Lemurians began to become more physical, their thought processes created a matching environmental structure. So too is it the case to say that the environmental fabric created the like-vibrational match within the beings that incarnated upon it.

We speak fully as if this process occurred in a linear way, yet it did not. The process appeared random, without pattern or structure. Yet in truth, there was much organisation.

The new physical bodies needed the higher amino acid profile and, as we said, the fruits that grew in the higher density did not translate into the physical density in the same way. Meat eating became necessary to sustain the physical body.

However, all is unified and the reason for one issue ties in with multiple reasons for multiple other issues. What we can say here is that the eating of the meat allowed the physical body to bind to the Earth reality and forget the higher connection. The consuming of the animal (a different form of other self in physicality) tied the individual into the hunter/hunted reality of consumption which is a service-to-self act, yet is at the same time in harmony with the new physical planet (if done correctly through selective choice of animal and ritualisation/blessing through ceremony).

The animals incarnation on the planet began to hold an energetic of extreme separation. They were able to herd together and create family, yet at the same time there was extreme conflict between them creating a hierarchical power struggle. You can see much of this today in your natural wildlife world. It became very much 'the survival of the fittest' if you will.

The humans at that time (mostly early Atlantean individuals yet some of these were the later Lemurians) connected in to the same frequencies of hierarchy and 'the survival of the fittest'. Eating meat and becoming the predator assisted them to connect into this field which, as we have said, was necessary for their growth.

Amongst all this were higher density positively polarised intelligences and 'lower density' negatively polarised intelligences, each influencing the energetic of the growing newly physical peoples on your planet.

These polarised intelligences were 'created by' the collective aligned and focused thought streams of the peoples upon Earth. So too were the peoples of Earth created by these polarised intelligences.

We speak indeed here of extraterrestrials (or ultra-dimensionals, they are actually one and the same from this perspective).

When you think of an 'extraterrestrial', many of you simply think of a being that lives upon another planet. This is indeed the case, but only from a linear perspective. The truth of the extraterrestrial intelligence is that they are formed by your collective consciousness when your planet moves into critical mass for focused thought. Yet these extraterrestrial intelligences are that which form you.

This is explained somewhat within our previous transmission *The Infinite Helix and the Emerald Flame* when we say your memories, when cohesive, form the field we call the 'eternal flame' or 'cosmic phire'. That field (known also as morphogenetic) is the fabric used for creation itself.

This is very much the same process. The higher intelligences (extraterrestrials) involved with your planet at that time were group souls known also as 'Logoi' or 'children of the Logos'.

There is a 'step down' in frequency from each group soul until all incarnating beings are 'children' of that particular Logos group soul. However, the incarnating beings must come together in harmonious, collective consciousness in order to create the Logos structure. These are simultaneous movements that move in perfect synchronisation. They are not linear. One does not come before the other. This is a convergence and that is how matter and antimatter structures are created. The convergence of structure.

The blueprint for the creation of these structures is that of the matrix system that we have presented in our previous transmissions.

We will continue to bring you the keys, codes and triggers for the cellular memories needed to fully merge with the matrix structures of creation that are all that is you. We shall do this within future transmissions.

This particular transmission has been specifically about what you consume.

As we said, the newly created Atlanteans, moving into an experience of free will and choice and thus separation, began to consume animal flesh. They were then able to key into the codes for the consuming or the taking of life in order to sustain themselves. This was not a choice they made, it was necessary to fuel their bodies optimally. The warrior energetic needed the full amino acid profile that the animal flesh provided.

There was no judgement here. It was part of the development of the fully physical human vehicle. The consuming of the life of the animal at that time became part of the programme.

However, there was much variation. In some areas of later Lemurian and early Atlantean times, they ate meat only when there was famine and they could not source other foodstuffs. Still there were many who lived fully plant-based, mostly those with Lemurian physiology who did not need meat to sustain their bodies. Although, as we have said, there was a little fish eating at the time.

The Lemurian and Atlantean times were 'time periods', not places. Although the humans at that time lived in certain areas across the planet, these are time periods as in 'ages' and within these ages were the civilisations or races that were the peoples.

As the Atlantean civilisations became more and more connected to the third density, they began to grow and expand through free will and choice as was the original plan. They began to show extreme intelligence as the 'extraterrestrial genetic keycodes' were switched on. They created amazing technologies and some of these technologies were part of their entire health and longevity. They were then able to choose what diets to follow and could sustain themselves with the aid of these advanced crystal technologies. The dietary plans followed by the later Atlanteans were as varied as they are in your today now moment. Some Atlanteans (reincarnated Lemurians) held the Lemurian memory codes for peace and harmony. The keys of compassion within them led them back to the fully plant-based diet plans and they had what you in your today would call 'superfoods'.

Other Lemurians (incarnating in from Sirius and also from the previous planet/age/timeline known as 'Marduk') held the warrior template and the memories for that. These individuals needed the meat from animals and their products because they were in complete aligned vibration to the consuming of the life force of another physical being. This brought with it the illusion of separation and thus choice and free will.

Do you see how there is no judgement here? The different physiology created by the paradigm of the individual and the memory structure of the soul itself is that which brought into alignment the consuming of animal flesh and by-product or the call to fully plant-based eating.

These beings, both Lemurian and Atlantean, were in what we call a 'fall phase' - their DNA was deconstructing itself from the 144 quantum code (infinite helix) through to the 12 strand ('beyond the triple helix' and 'triple helix') and down into the double helix configuration. This is extremely simplified as many souls incarnated in from different densities with different memory structure and thus different DNA strand configurations, but this gives you somewhat of a picture as to how it was.

Many physical structures needed to consume other living life forms in order to create/align with the environmental energetic frequency of the fall phase they were in. The natural and the organic were also hijacked and false environmental systems were put in place. Outside of the scope of this particular transmission, yet you can see how extremely multifaceted and convoluted the presentation of reality was at this time. This multifaceted convolution remains into your today now moment. However, there is a difference and that difference is most large.

You are now currently in a 'climb phase'. Your frequencies are moving upwards into reconstruction, not downwards into deconstruction.

Many, many Lemurian and Atlantean souls have reincarnated over and over (some through choice in complete service and others through getting caught in the reincarnational pattern through the law of karma and the hijacked trapping systems) and they are incarnated upon your planet in your today now moment.

Lemurians did not have the technology to consciously project themselves into future incarnations, yet they had a window into the potential of what those incarnations may be. The Atlanteans did not have the extremely unified insight of the Lemurians, yet they were able to develop the technologies needed to project themselves into future lifetimes (death to birth conscious transfer). This is simply the creation of a future incarnation from the conscious intentional focus of the previous life, rather than the creation of it from the higher dimensional aspect after that soul has left the physical body.

We speak here again very generally and in a most basic way as there were many overlaps and nuances within the Lemurian/Atlantean pattern. At one point, the Lemurian/Atlantean societies were merged as one until they began to migrate to different areas as the geological templates of the land changed.

The Lemurians and the Atlanteans were very different and when in conflict, the Atlantean focus overwhelmed the peaceful and softer Lemurian race. Yet many Atlanteans realised the Lemurian peoples were gifted in ways they could not conceive of. Some Atlanteans became jealous of the Lemurian abilities and others valued them and loved them dearly.

Upon your planet in your today now moment, the genetic traits of the Lemurian and the Atlantean presentations remain, exist and flourish within the starseeds.

We can liken the Lemurian genetic template to the individuals you may know as 'crystal'.

We can liken the Atlantean genetic template to the individuals you may know as 'indigo'.

Although this is a basic presentation of individualised and complex fields, this does go someway to explaining the magnetic pull (or ancient keycodes no longer serving you) towards consuming either an animal-based diet or a plant-based diet.

The crystal individuals, like the Lemurians, will be drawn towards the vegan lifestyle. The indigo individuals will be drawn towards consuming animal flesh and products. However, this is a generalisation for you are each a combination of these frequencies. Yet there is often a predominance of one or the other.

We shall explain further, but we may add that when we talk about the Lemurians and Atlanteans consuming animal flesh, we are not talking about the factory farmed animals that you consume upon your planet today.

Even in the times of battle amongst the Atlantean races, the animals were appropriately fed and taken care of. We are not saying there was never cruelty and that animals did not suffer in those times. Yet this was nothing compared to the large scale that occurs upon your planet today.

We return now to the subject of the indigo and crystal individuals.

8: The Rainbow Warrior Code

Remembering that a fully whole foods and plant-based diet is perfectly in alignment for accelerated or stargate ascension, we give here a very basic template of how this may be implemented within the framework of the crystal and the indigo energies for the overall ascension path.

The fully plant-based diet when whole, fresh, closest to its origin and grown in nutrient-rich soil without chemical sprays is most suited to the predominantly crystal individual.

The reason for this is because the fully plant-based diet creates peace, compassion and relaxation within the body. There are warming foods with more fire, cooling foods with more peaceful, relaxing qualities or spicier/high energy foods with a stimulating quality. Yet overall, the plant-based diet, when followed/chosen correctly and in alignment in the way we have explained, promotes a peaceful countenance within.

Crystal individuals are natural healers and spend time 'going within' to just be. They sense energy naturally. Like the Lemurians, they do not need to explain the energy they sense or analyse it, they simply work with it.

The crystal energetic is most similar to the Lemurian energetic. Many reincarnated Lemurians have called to themselves a physical body of the crystal vibration.

A diet still rich in plant foods but containing smaller quantities of sustainably and ethically raised meat, seafood, eggs and goat/sheep dairy, when whole and fresh and chemical/toxin-free is most suited to the indigo individual.

The eating of the animal flesh allows the indigo to take in full amino acid profile foods and connect into the 'consuming of other physical beings' energy so that they may activate the warrior code within. The indigo individuals are natural system busters, rising against oppression, fighting for the cause. Like the Atlanteans, they are analytical and extremely creative. They are often writers and public speakers. They have no problem being 'out there', unlike the crystal individuals who crave anonymity.

The indigo energetic is most similar to the Atlantean energetic. Many reincarnated Atlanteans have called to themselves a physical body of the indigo vibration.

However, all we have said here is a very basic and generalised template. The nuances in-between explain the vast differences between incarnated physical individuals.

The 'climb phase' energy that you currently experience in your today now moment is a moving from carbon-based (which craves animal flesh) into crystalline-based (which is sustained by light).

Each and every starseed is moving in the direction of the crystalline, regardless of overall energetic signature being crystal or indigo.

There are also those incarnated upon the violet ray, the blue ray and the rose ray. So too are there others. Together you make up the 'rainbow children' or indeed the 'rainbow warriors'. Regardless of what you consume, you are rainbow warriors.

We refer to you as 'starseeds' due to the fact that you are 'from the stars' and that you literally 'seed the stars' (explained in *The Infinite Helix and the Emerald Flame*).

Yet when your collective energy fields are viewed from the quantum, higher perspective, together you make up the most beautiful and perfect rainbow. You are standing up for that which is just, you are indeed justice warriors. You are standing up for truth, you are indeed truth warriors. Together you make up the rainbow, you are absolutely and completely 'rainbow warriors'.

The clue here regarding your diet therefore is in your vibration.

Collectively you are the rainbow and this is that which is most best, most highest and most in alignment to eat, that of your rainbow. The deep colours within the fruits and the vegetables are that which contain the codes you need for the job at hand.

So therefore, if you are a fully plant-based eater, ensure that the food is wholesome and unchanged (closest to its origin as possible) and ensure you consume all the colours of the rainbow.

If you do consume animal flesh and their products, then ensure they are sustainably and ethically raised and humanely killed.

Bless the animal and give it thanks at every meal. Ritualise this in the ways of the warrior. Make sure that the predominant foodstuffs you take in make up the rainbow.

These are simply the ways forward. There is much contention regarding the different dietary regimes on your planet, yet the ultimate truth is the eating of the rainbow. If you hold fast to this as you gather the food then you will be following the path of the starseed, the ascending one and the rainbow warrior. The Lemurian diet is your basic template and the rainbow is that which you build as you create the cleansing and the nourishing path before you.

Regarding the crystal and the indigo frequencies as basic template, we give you some potential scenarios. As you read these words, you feel into the scenario and see if it resonates with you. If it does, then this is a clue to your most aligned eating style.

Many of you do not need these presentations for resonation. You already follow the conscious eating style and the information you receive within this transmission is purely for the purposes of confirmation.

Yet for those who need the presentations in order to align and strengthen the resonance within, we present these example scenarios through the templates of crystal and indigo.

These are basic and fictional templates presented as a teaching tool for your personal alignment and inner knowing.

Example 1: Melinda

Melinda is a crystal individual. She is fully vegan. Melinda suffers from extreme anxiety. Despite the many and varied reasons for her anxiety, Melinda may benefit from introducing some animal products into her diet. The reason for this is that her vegan diet, mostly raw, is very cleansing. The animal products will bring in the nourishment she is looking for.

Melinda may find that as an anxious person, the flesh and milk of land-based animals may push her anxiety into a more extreme state. Therefore she would be most assisted by bringing in eggs and some fish into her eating plan. This detour into nourishment need not be permanent. After a time (possibly months, certainly no longer than a couple of years), Melinda will have attained the balance she is looking for and she can return to full plant-based eating.

We are not saying that the nourishing path cannot be found through the eating of animal products only. The plant-based path can be most nourishing. Yet we present this potential scenario for the crystal individual who may find him or herself in this place.

Example 2: Richard

Richard is a crystal individual. He eats a diet of sustainably raised meats, fish and animal products alongside plant foods. He suffers also from extreme anxiety along with some physical health issues. Richard follows a nourishing diet plan. Richard may benefit from eliminating all animal products and becoming fully plant-based with a high amount of the plant foods consumed raw. Richard builds the rainbow upon his plate. This plant-based plan may become a permanent lifestyle plan for Richard or could be temporary. Richard has moved into the deeply detoxifying and cleansing diet and reaps the benefits of this.

Example 3: Alison

Alison is an indigo individual. She eats healthily, following a plant-based plus seafood diet plan. She has reversed health issues and emotional issues in her life and continues to enjoy good health. Alison begins to have memories of other lifetimes. She remembers living as a peaceful, magickal being who ate plant foods only. She begins to feel terrible guilt about eating fish and seafood, yet is worried if she stops eating this that it will effect her current good health. Alison is an individual holding a 'vegan philosophy' yet her indigo physical body is craving seafood. Alison is therefore in a conflicting energy state and this potentially puts out a mixed vibration into the creative, etheric energy field around her, presenting mixed experiences and challenges in her life.

The issue here is not necessarily with Alison's eating pattern but with the guilt she now feels by consuming that seafood. The memories of living a fully compassionate life as a plant-based eater become stronger and stronger as she raises her vibration.

Alison has two choices. She can either work on the issues of guilt, giving thanks, gratitude and blessings to the life of the sea creatures she is eating or she can remove seafood from her diet and replace it with other foodstuffs that hold a similar energy. If Alison chooses to remain as a pescatarian then she needs to do this with complete and utter peace and alignment. If she chooses this path, she may need assistance from the crystal healer individuals around her (counsellor, naturopath, psychic reader, energy worker, and so on) but finding the acceptance with her eating style is more important to the overall energy system of the individual than the actual foodstuffs eaten.

If Alison chooses to move to a fully plant-based diet then she needs to work upon the 'fear of becoming ill if she gives up fish' and move into the plant-based diet with the full knowing that this is the best, most aligned way for her to eat.

At first, it would be most helpful to bring in the seafood replacement. We do not speak here of the mock, processed foodstuffs available on your planet which are fractionated, unnatural foods that the physical body cannot place and categorise within; we speak here of sea vegetables.

Eating the seaweeds will connect her with the energy of the sea that she has been used to consuming. She would then need to replace the fats which are the ready converted essential fatty acids found in the fish. The algae is one choice. She can then begin to consume the precursors to the essential fatty acids. We speak here of that which you call the 'omega-3' and the 'ALA' which converts to the EPA and DHA.

These are very basic presentations of these fatty acids but an abundant intake of the rainbow plant materials will assist in the absorption of these fatty acids. There is much information available upon your planet on this issue and much is accurate.

We would add to this that once on a fully plant-based diet, a healthy human body will convert more of the precursor than those that consume the seafoods. We would say in order to aid this conversion, lean towards the precursor ALA foods of the omega-3 variety more than the omega-6. The balance can be found.

We speak of your oils here, which are fractionated also and not fully whole foods. However, if extracted from the plant as cleanly as is possible then these are helpful transitionary stopgaps or permanent backups as you find your way.

So Alison can choose that which is in alignment for her. She can always choose to return to the pescatarian diet plan if she finds that the fully plant-based plan is not working for her. The emotional issues of the guilt and the fear are that which to take note of as priority.

Example 4: Mitchell

Mitchell is an indigo individual. Mitchell is fully plant-based eating a rainbow diet of fresh fruits and vegetables, including the essential fat foods such as avocado and coconut. Mitchell has suffered a few health issues which are greatly assisted by following the plant-based diet. However, he has been told by a holistic therapist to consider bringing in some animal products in his diet. Mitchell feels he cannot do this and is a fully rooted ethical vegan. He absolutely wishes to remain vegan and has no intention of consuming any kind of animal product. Mitchell is a spiritually aware starseed, raising his vibration into the crystalline form.

Mitchell holds a strong vegan philosophy, yet his physiology is missing something. If Mitchell were to consume animal products, this would place him in an emotionally conflicted state and his intuition tells him it is not the way for him to bless the animal or come to terms with consuming the animal product. Therefore, if it is fully in alignment for Mitchell to make a change but NOT move into the consuming of the animal product, what can he do?

Firstly we would suggest Mitchell bring in the seaweeds and sea vegetables connecting him to the sea. His current plan is very cleansing so we would direct him towards the nourishing foods, yet he is already consuming the avocados and the coconuts. We would suggest he continue to consume these yet also look to fattier fruits such as olives and more exotic fatty fruits. We would suggest he consume the nuts, the seeds and the berries. Yet Mitchell needs something more.

The area for him to look towards is to the herbs, the rare mushrooms and the superfoods. Some of these are to be found upon your planet as fractionated or powders, but in the case of an indigo individual (whose physiology may lean more towards needing animal products but whose philosophy is fully plant-based) then these fractionated superfoods and powders are indeed useful.

The Lemurians had many exotic fruits, vegetables, seeds, roots and shoots that held an abundance of everything that they needed physiologically, even for a long time after the fall. As you begin the climb and return to the Lemurian consciousness, despite your indigo vibration, the way to emulate the dietary plan the Lemurians consumed is to look to the high nutrient foods you call 'superfoods'.

There is much available upon your planet regarding these superfoods and we need not move into an area already so widely covered as much is accurate. We would encourage you to source the best quality of these fractionated foods and powders that you can.

So Mitchell chooses to upgrade his diet from fully plant-based, into fully plant-based with supplementation through superfoods. He is then able to sustain optimum health through the vegan lifestyle he so resonates with. There are a great many indigo starseeds who resonate with this example of Mitchell.

Example 5: Tracey

Tracey is indigo and feels that she is a starseed warrior for truth. She eats a high plant diet with the addition of ethically sourced meats primarily from game such as rabbit or deer. She hunts some of this food herself and consumes roadkill and other wild animal flesh foods. She has her own smallholding with her own chickens, ducks, pigs and goats. She looks after these animals well and consumes their eggs, milk and meat.

Tracey feels no guilt and happily exists in a reciprocal, harmonious relationship with the animals she lives with and looks after. She is a spiritually aware individual.

If Tracey provides a compassionate life, and end to life, for the animals she raises and feels that she is in alignment with this lifestyle then there is no judgement from her higher self or the higher realms for this. Each starseed is valued and honoured. Tracey would be respected for sourcing her own animal foodstuffs rather than purchasing animal foods already killed by another.

Tracey exists in her own harmonious ecosystem most similar to that of the indigenous peoples. She is 'in a contract' if you will, with the animals she cares for (from the higher perspective).

She can look to this contractual agreement in a far more physical sense, for she is literally fulfilling it in every way by caring for the animals. The animals do not move into resistance as they are killed, as Tracey ensures this is done with the least possible suffering to the animals that she genuinely loves. This is a very different form of love for animals than one holding a 'vegan philosophy' has, yet it is indeed genuine love for the animals.

It is simply a different path and if one is going to consume animal flesh, this would be the way to do it whilst creating as little karma as possible. The killing of the animal always creates karma and we cannot say this way of living would be creating a neutralised balance that is totally 'karma-free', as is that of the plant-based eater. However, when it comes to the consuming of animals then this would be the closest one could get to a balanced karmic state.

Example 6: Lucy

Lucy is an indigo individual who is very psychic and empathic. She is able to channel and communicate with her higher guidance structure system and with various non-physical entities. Lucy holds a vegan philosophy and follows a vegan lifestyle. After experiencing some health issues, Lucy decides to incorporate some sustainably raised fish into her diet. However, Lucy quickly discovers that the eating of this fish affects her ability to connect cleanly and easily to the higher guidance system. Lucy therefore goes back to a plant-based diet and, like the previous example of Mitchell, she brings in the superfood supplementation and the sea vegetables to add balance to her diet while remaining plant-based.

What is happening here is the vibrational signal of the fish is interfering with the crystalline broadcast of the signal of the fifth dimension. The fish binds one to the fourth dimension so it is easier to assimilate psychically than the animal flesh yet for someone as psychic and clairvoyant as Lucy, she can feel the interference.

The Lucy example is occurring currently within your now moment reality for a great many starseeds. As you raise your vibrational frequency, you can no longer align with the binding to the signals of the third and fourth dimensions. You crave the aligned balance of the fully anchored pillar of light, vertical axis as the foundation template for your matrix architecture.

Many highly psychic and sensitive ascending starseeds can literally feel the energy of the animal they have just consumed. For a sensitive starseed to consume factory farmed animal flesh, it can be extremely distressing. They can feel the pain and the suffering of the animal and witness flashing, horrific visual images of the life that animal lived. When it comes to consuming fish, they feel as though they are choking or cannot breathe, on an energetic level.

The aware, trained, anchored and balanced starseed can transmute this experience so they may continue to consume meat or fish. Yet even the most adept at this transmutation will feel some connection to the animal and, as we have said previously, no amount of blessing or giving thanks from one person can alter or neutralise the suffering the animal experienced within a third dimensional level.

For the majority of starseeds able to tune in and feel the vibrations of the animal's suffering, the choice for them is to move to plant-based eating. When eating plants, due to the natural acceptance of the plant's shift from one state to another, there is no suffering for the psychic or empathic individual to feel. Only joy and the high energy created by consuming a species appropriate foodstuff.

This sensitivity stretches into other substances such as medications, caffeine, sugar and processed, denatured foodstuffs.

The reason for this is that the sensitive, empathic and psychic individual (these traits do not always go together, but often do) can feel energy regardless of whether that energy is directly in front of them, in another room, another country, on another planet or in another universe.

Energy is non-locational, it is everywhere and it is where you are. The reason for this is that you are an infinite being and you are all things.

So a psychic starseed can feel energy no matter where it may be. They can even more closely feel energy that is actually consumed by them and is taken into the body.

This can also be the same transdermally (injections, vaccinations, skin cream products, oils, perfumes) which works for healing and benefit when it comes to aromatherapy or magnesium or other healing remedies.

This brings us now to a different way that the individual takes in etheric energy through physical substance. We speak here of the sexual act between couples.

9: Goddess Kali, Liquid Light and Sex Magick

The female womb is a receptacle, a vessel. Like a cup (or chalice), it holds, nurtures, contains and incubates. This is its purpose.

Each female's womb holds a consciousness and an intelligence itself. Like another 'woman' living within the physical body of the female. 'She' would be the archetype of the 'dark goddess' or the 'goddess Kali'.

The womb is the 'sacred zero-point within', if you will.

Due to the fact that the female is a natural receptacle and 'holds' energy then the ascending female would work to transmute energy that she receives. This works on all levels spiritually, psychologically, emotionally and physically.

On a physical level, the female literally 'receives' physical energy from the male during the act of sex.

A highly sensitive and psychic female can feel and 'take in' energetic frequency from the physical substance received from the male. Therefore if you are an ascending plant-based eating female who has a sexual partner that eats factory farmed meat (or consumes alcohol, tobacco, sugar, man-made mind-altering substances, chemicals and so on) then the 'energy' of these substances are delivered into the physical body of the female through the sexual act.

This puts the highly sensitive, ascending, starseed female in a challenging position. One cannot force one's partner to change their lifestyle habits, so what does the female do in this situation?

Some starseed females may choose to align with a male who follows the same lifestyle and eating patterns that they do, and be most strict in that criteria when selecting a mate. Yet this is not always the case for that female.

A choice may be to present to the male a desire for him to change his lifestyle and eating habits but, as we have said, this cannot be done through force. A male may decide that eating meat or consuming tobacco and so on is part of his reality that he chooses to embrace.

The female could choose to use a barrier method within the sexual act to ensure no physical substance is taken into the body. However, there are three issues with this...

1) Every act of physical love between a couple is an energy exchange so even without the receiving of the physical substance, one still aligns oneself with the energy field of the partner (to a lesser extent).

2) The receiving of the male physical substance, when in energetic alignment with that male, is a trigger into attaining higher consciousness and Kundalini activation. It is the receiving of 'liquid light' as Kali, the dark goddess, utilises the liquid light substance as a powerful creative force for manifestation on all levels.

3) The couple have decided to create a child between them. Whilst the creation on a physical level results in a child for that couple, the sexual exchange (and especially the receiving of the liquid light) is a seed point into many different creative aspects and outcomes. This energetic working between aligned frequency couples is known upon your planet as 'tantric creation' or 'sex magick'.

As we have said, the most aligned situation here would be for both partners to be embracing similar lifestyles and paradigms as they ascend in balance as part of a twin flame union.

However, this is not always the case as many unions sit within a twin flame 'potential' or move in and out of a twin flame pattern. This does not mean that you are not supposed to be with your mate or that you have chosen the wrong mate. Each of you move through your ascension and awakening journeys at a different pace, reaching different stages at different times.

The differences between the partners are often the greatest triggers into their own personal growth and this supposed or perceived 'mismatch' is actually part of the twin flame union as they are mirrors and catalysts for each other.

The act of compassion, unconditional love and compromise (or the creation of the 'divine contract' which is the true marriage) is catalysed by differences between the partners within the relationship as they move into that masculine/feminine balance. The relationship itself taking on its own life force and becoming its own entity in its own right. That entity having existed long before the couple met within their physical lives. In this case, they are 'partners of destiny'.

So in the case of the female who is in a destined, twin flame potential relationship with their divine male counterpart, who chooses a different lifestyle path to their mate, the way forward here is to practice transmutation of energy.

The male, whilst still undergoing the energetic exchange during the act of sex, does not hold energetic frequency in the same way as he is a 'giver' of energy. However, some spiritual work may need to be undertaken here for ultimately the male is giving energy to Kali (the dark goddess) who can be unpredictable. The male needs to be fully aware of who he is giving energy to and be in a state of complete trust and surrender as he gives that precious life force of liquid light to his mate. It is therefore just as important for the male to share his sexual experiences with a female of like-vibration as it is the female, even though he does not receive or hold energy.

So, regarding the female. How does she receive the liquid light, utilise her tantric connection with her mate as trigger/catalyst into visionary states, Kundalini and enlightenment and transmute the energies that are not in alignment?

More to the point, is the female still holding energy from past relationships, or situations of sexual abuse? The answer to this may well be yes, depending on the energetic development of that female.

Many incarnated females hold on to stagnant, stale and unwanted energy that no longer serves them. Sometimes for years, sometimes a lifetime (and carries the energy through to other lifetimes).

Also, 'quantum versions' (alternate selves, other choices you could have made) can hold stagnant energy even when you, yourself, are clear. Remember here, this is Kali, the dark goddess. She is highly creative (the physical vessel to grow and nurture a child) on all levels, she is mysterious and magickal. She is indeed to be honoured and, when clear and in alignment, she is a beautiful, wondrous being to behold. She stands as the powerful shadow divine feminine.

She can also flip into her negative aspect if too much stagnant energy builds up. She can be manipulative, secretive (rather than private) and she can be as much the destroyer (taker of life) as that of the creatrix (giver of life).

A great majority of third dimensional incarnated females hold so much trauma within the womb energy centre that they manifest (in varying degrees) the negative aspect of Kali. This presents as the manipulative female, the subservient female, the passive-aggressive female or the archetype you call 'extreme feminist'. All these are distortions of the true divine feminine and are the negative aspects of Kali.

Many women present as the soft, yielding, receptive female. Yet when they are triggered, their trauma comes to the fore (most often without them realising) and they become the negative manifestation of Kali.

However, we speak here of third dimensional females.

The starseed females undergoing an ascension process are much different. They are on a journey, which we can present as an ascending incline (although in truth it is a sine wave or spiral).

We are not saying all ascending starseed females are fully clear and never flip into the negative aspect of Kali. What we are saying here is that the traumas held within the sacred womb centre become known to the female as she works through traumas on all levels. As she embraces fifth dimensional consciousness, she becomes multidimensional and quantum and begins to work with all the aspects of herself. An ascending starseed woman becomes aware of the divine feminine within her.

However, many starseeded females, aware of a multitude of archetypal goddess presentations, are not always aware of Kali. She is the shadow, mysterious and hidden, often to the female and to the other archetypal presentations of the divine feminine.

Some ascending females choose to reject Kali whilst embracing the archetypal light goddess presentations. This leads to an imbalance and also the potential for the negative aspect of Kali to present. That which you reject through resistance is thus given more power. *What you resist persists.*[3]

This is not only confusing to the incarnated female as to who she is as she focuses on a spiritual life, unfolding before her an ascension and enlightenment experience, but it is also confusing and frustrating for the male who is her partner.

Incarnated males do not hold such a multitude of archetypal presentations within their make-up. Traumas are held differently and present in a much more direct way when triggered (such as anger, fury and aggression). It is challenging for the male to interact with the negative aspect of Kali, for it is Kali (the divine feminine mystery) that they are attracted to. The positive aspect of Kali is the most seductive aspect of the woman. This is as it should be for it ensures reproduction of the human race on Earth. Yet negative Kali pushes the male away and the male sees her as a threat. Manipulation, passive-aggressive behaviour or extreme feminism are abhorrent to the balanced ascending male.

We would say to these males that pointing out the presentation of negative Kali to your partner is not always the most aligned way forward in your relationship. This can trigger the traumas within the female even more. Although some ascending females within an extremely harmonious and trusting relationship can respond to this being made aware of by the male, depending on how the male presents the awareness of negative Kali. This must

---

3   Carl Gustav Jung, psychiatrist and psychoanalyst, famously contended that "what you resist not only persists, but will grow in size." This viewpoint is generally abbreviated to "what you resist persists."

be presented within an accepting and supportive energy and not an accusatory one.

When negative Kali appears, she has been triggered through fear and trauma. She is looking for love, healing and balance. The appearance of negative Kali that repels you so much is the time your mate most needs your love.

The big question to ask yourself here is whether there is growth within your partner. Does she acknowledge her own traumas? Is she working upon them? Do you see wisdom, love and expansion within your female? If the answer to these questions are yes, then you can be assured that she is working with her Kali aspect. She is in a state of transmutation and balance.

The female must not be made to feel bad or wrong because negative Kali has shown herself. Most especially when that woman is transmuting traumas within and working with all the multitude of divine feminine archetypes that she holds.

However, if the answer to these questions are no, and if your female partner is consistently presenting as the negative Kali aspect, then she is not moving through transmutation and integration. You will find thus your relationship to be a challenge.

There are many ways that an ascending female can transmute the womb energy centre, move through the long-held stagnant energies of trauma and work with Kali to integrate her positive aspect.

The positive aspect of Kali is creative, wise, mysterious, nurturing and loving. She is a master healer and the inner mother (the creator of matter).

The traumas held within (which are triggers/catalysts to the negative Kali) can manifest as physical illness and disease of the ovaries, womb and cervix. When these traumas clear and positive Kali is integrated, then the physical female organs become clear and healthy.

It is important for a woman to 'cycle with the moon' or with her 'soul star sisters' and to accept her stage of life. Be this menstruation, perimenopause or postmenopause (the maiden, mother, crone journey embracing the 'wise woman' at each stage). Rejection or resistance to each of these stages of life can create stagnant energy, fresh trauma, trigger old traumas and give rise to negative Kali.

Infertility can be a result of too much stagnant build up within the womb centre. When a woman works to clear the sexual traumas and become clear and healthy, then she will conceive a child (If this is in her pre-incarnate blueprint or choice to do so).

These we present are standardisations and generalisations. Each incarnated female is vastly different and, as we have said, holds a multitude of archetypal divine presentations of the feminine. Kali herself is a multidimensional goddess being.

Yet it is the case that a majority of incarnated females do hold trauma within the womb centre. This is changing rapidly within young females born into starseed families as they nurture their daughters within all aspects of their development. Also, the integration of indigo and crystal aspects within the starseed females creates a release of these traumas and we see the positive aspect of Kali flourish for the first time upon your planet since the times of Lemuria and Atlantis.

Kali herself has been manipulated and hijacked. The depth and breadth of this manipulation is beyond the scope of this transmission. However, the information templates regarding the hijacking sits within the realm you know as 'Akash' (Akashic records) and is 'downloaded' into the memory fields of the awakened and ascending individuals continuously.

These downloads are not always interpreted in balance, but they are coming into the awareness of your peoples. This is that which triggers the 'liberty templates' to come online (which is the same thing as saying that the ancient stargates are opening).

This is a vast story and indeed our role is to present this story to you. We have done this and shall continue to do this. Each of you, once having received these downloads, can also build a picture of the story of Gaia's transition through the light levels of descension and ascension (the cosmic sine wave or spiral).

The immunity to hijacking and becoming the master of your own matrix that we present within the transmission *Masters of the Matrix* is a transmission that assists you to transmute energy (as a female, male or neutrally presenting gender-free individual).

Therefore if you are looking to transmute long-held stagnant womb energy and present the Kali goddess archetype in her positive presentation, then the work within *Masters of the Matrix* will assist. However, the work presented there is sixth dimensional (sacred geometric archetypal form).

A fifth dimensional presentation may be more in alignment for many females. The meditations within the *Masters of the Matrix* material are fifth dimensional and these can be used for this work.

Yet we present here a specific meditation that works upon the long-held traumas within the womb centre. The meditation works regarding holding on to energy from past relationships and trauma experiences that no longer serve you. Yet this meditation will not clear from you energy that *does* still serve you. (See Chapter 13, "The Golden Chalice")

The womb, as we have said, is a receptacle and holds energy (as the golden chalice). It is important for the female to know that *it is perfectly in alignment to hold on to energy, if that energy serves you in your now.*

For example, carrying a child to term is holding on to an energy that serves you. Holding on to the liquid light given to you from your mate during your tantric sexual act is also holding on to an energy that serves you.

If you are wishing to transmute the liquid light given to you from your mate, due to the fact that his lifestyle choices do not align with yours, then this meditation will work to clear that. You may need to do this meditation many times in order to continuously transmute. As we have said, this is not the ideal. But as each of you are on your own journeys, it may be necessary for many females to do this.

So if your mate is fully in alignment with you, this meditation will allow you to hold on to that liquid light for your creative and magickal tantric work.

If your mate is not fully in alignment with your lifestyle choices, then you will transmute and clear the liquid light. This does not mean you cannot utilise the liquid light for magickal work, it simply means that you 'take the light aspect that you need' and you transmute the rest.

The filtering has been done for you. You need not be aware on a conscious level which aspects are transmuted and cleared and which are held on to. Many of you will be aware of this but you do not need to be. This meditation has been formulated and created exactly to transmute that which needs transmuting and to retain energy that serves you.

We will present this meditation, 'The Golden Chalice', at the end of this transmission. We would like to draw your attention also to other tools that can be used for transmutation of the womb centre traumas, energy that does not align and the presentation of the negative Kali archetype.

The first is yoga. We speak here of the practise of asanas. There are many styles of yoga that will work to transmute this energy. If you practise yoga regularly or if you teach yoga yourself, then it is highly likely that you have transmuted this energy already. However, if the trauma runs deep then the energetic imprints can return after the yoga session. For deep traumas, then multiple tools often need to be engaged.

Transmutation of a tantric partner's liquid light energy that you receive is very likely to be worked with effectively through regular yoga.

There are other Eastern styles of movement that can also assist with this transmutation. They would work with movement that engages the sacral chakra.

Chakra meditation. Working with cleansing of all the chakras, most especially the sacral chakra would be transmutative to that which we speak of.

Crystal work and crystal healing. You would be looking to use orange coloured crystals in this work. Simply wearing orange or amber coloured crystal jewellery works to transmute the womb energy centre and to allow the positive Kali energy to flourish.

Goddess or moon workshops and ceremonies. These ceremonies of women who gather together work specifically regarding all that we present here. If you feel you need to work with the balance of the divine feminine, release sexual trauma and present the positive Kali archetype then these workshops are most in alignment. Use your intuition on this, however. These workshops must be led by a 'high priestess'. This does not mean someone who has taken some kind of certification course or achieved that title by some given organisation. The title of 'high priestess' is given by universal and cosmic forces (although the physical organisations can be in alignment with this, but not always). The 'high priestess' is she who presents balanced and multidimensional presentations of the numerous and plentiful goddess archetypes, including the shadow aspect of Kali in her positive aspect.

Massage. Full body massage, paying attention to sacral chakra/womb area is extremely successful in transmutation of this energy. Using high quality oils draws out the impurities and working with crystals at the same time creates even more healing power. Choose again most carefully as you utilise discretion and discernment. You would be looking for a massage therapist with a high light quotient who has herself balanced these energies. This therapist would be 'spiritually aware' if you will. There are many females drawn to massage therapy who are themselves in need of this transmutative work. If a woman who presents her Kali archetype through the negative aspect works on you as your massage therapist then this would potentially have the opposite effect! Choose your therapist wisely and carefully.

There is much light, love and awareness within your lightworker, starseed and healing communities. Yet there is also distortion and infiltration. Your discernment and intuition is needed muchly when choosing to align yourself with others for magickal and healing work.

On this subject, we might mention that some crystal practitioners advocate placing crystals inside the vagina in order to accomplish crystal healing work. We would present to you that we <u>do not</u> advocate this work. The crystal energy is to be placed upon the sacral chakra so it moves down into the womb. The crystals can also be worn upon the body as jewellery, as we have said, with intention for their healing/balancing/communication. Placing crystals inside the vagina does not reach the womb energy in the correct alignment and could be detrimental or harmful to the female.

There are cases where douches, liquids or herbs can be used in specific healings. Again, you would use your intuition in this sense.

Tantric work with your twin flame partner can, in itself, be a form of healing from past traumas. If you are with a partner who aligns with your lifestyle choices and you are able to retain his liquid light, then together the two of you would envisage the liquid light to be filling your womb to the point that no other energy can exist there. You would together create a unique magickal working for this, but this alone can be enough to transmute all previous negative and stagnant energies and long-held traumas from your womb.

Does this mean that aligning with the twin flame partner can, in and of itself, draw out the positive aspect of goddess Kali? Indeed, this is exactly what this means.

Masturbation and self-pleasure. When this is done for magickal reasons, this can be also most effective. This is for the female who is not in a relationship or who utilises this work as part of her relationship. Whilst you would not be taking in the physical liquid light, you can still use masturbation as a tool for cleansing, clearing and transmutation. We would suggest that you are aware of the energies created here, for too much indulgence in self-pleasure can have the opposite effect and create the negative aspect of Kali.

Masturbation can also be utilised as a healing tool, most especially during menstruation, to ease pressure, pain and to encourage flow.

Foods and nutrition. The Lemurian diet we present here within this transmission is, in and of itself, a healing, cleansing and nourishing diet. The predominantly whole food, plant-based female will naturally be cleansing all organs within her body through her nutrition. However, in conjunction with other magickal work, we would suggest the partaking of the red and orange foods.

To create a blend of red fruits (such as berries and cherries) or to eat the radishes, beetroots, red apples and tomatoes with specific intention for this womb energy work creates much healing power.

There are other superfoods and herbs that work on the sacral chakra, womb and feminine organs. Look for a master teacher upon your planet or a spiritually aware nutritional practitioner who can work with you to achieve this balance through foods and herbs. The flower remedies and homeopathic blends also work on this level. Place the intention to meet the master healer or teacher, and that teacher shall come into your life.

The meditation presented at the end of this transmission, 'The Golden Chalice', is specifically for incarnated females.

However, the transgender female may also benefit from this meditation. Whilst the transgender female does not hold a physical womb, the genuine transgender female will hold an 'etheric' womb. She will therefore hold on to energy in a similar way to a biologically born female.

This is a hugely vast subject and far outside the scope of this transmission. There is much hijacking and distortion here. However, from the higher dimensional perspective, there are those who have chosen a life path where they experience living as the physical gender that is in opposition to the gender identity they hold. These individuals have a different soul blueprint and they will hold an etheric aspect of themselves that is the presentation of their gender identity. In this case, this would be their 'true identity' or 'soul identity' (this does not mean the soul itself holds a gender for it is genderless).

As you move through the raise in frequency, there has been much put in place to prevent that raise and activation within you. This is the creation of the inverted matrix. Many of these black box programmes have been put into place. Within our transmission *The Black Box Programme and the Rose Gold Flame as Antidote*, we presented information on vaccines, chemtrails and other chemical and energetic warfare.[4] There are other 'black box programmes' that exist within different bandwidth fields of the inverted matrix.

Gender confusion is one of these programmes, as this prevents the rise of the divine feminine and the sacred masculine in harmony and balance. Yet the ultimate aim of this particular black box programme is division of humanity.

As we have said, there are 'genuine' transgender individuals who have incarnated to experience this and their collective mission is to raise the awareness of humanity towards the galactic diversity and presentation of the different expressions of gender. Throughout your galactic multiverse, the expressions of gender are beyond your imaginings at this point. Therefore the genuine transgender individuals have also had their divine mission 'hijacked', if you will.

It is challenging for many of you who are aware of the black box programme for gender confusion to accept anything other than pure distortion when it comes to a transgender individual. Yet so too are many of you unable to accept anything other than pure distortion when it comes to the extraterrestrial presence. Yet both of these are hijacked inverse creations that hold the positive aspect also.

Regarding the transgender female, you may find one individual expressing a full manifestation of 'negative Kali' in her darkest form. Yet you may find another transgender individual who presents as 'positive Kali', embracing the divine feminine in a *more balanced* way than a biological female! There is no one community or group that is the product of hijacking or that is fully negative, distorted or dark. There is darkness and light in all

---

4   "The Black Box Programme and the Rose Gold Flame as Antidote" (2019)
      by Magenta Pixie

groups and communities. One must use intuition when one meets the individual, for each individual is an infinity unto itself.

As we have said, this is a vast and deeply nuanced subject and we have touched on it in the briefest of ways here. Remember, the ultimate aims of the hijacking and all black box programmes are the *division of humanity.* Why? Because the division of humanity leads to an inability to create the critical mass needed for the various stages of the energetic raise and the ascension.

We might add that these black box programmes are shutting down as more and more of humanity become aware of them. They depend on being 'hidden' in order to work effectively. Once they are 'seen', they begin to break down and cease to function.

The division of humanity has indeed occurred on your planet and is still occurring. Yet it is not enough to prevent critical mass for the energetic light raise, DNA activation and ascension.

The critical mass has been reached in many areas and the core (known as the 'red spider') of the inverted matrix has broken down and ceased to exist. At the time of this transmission, in your year of 2019, the inverted matrix is being sustained through 'backup generators' which are the various black box programmes. The core (red spider) cannot be reconstructed due to critical mass for fifth strand activation and the 'Emerald Flame Activation' having been reached upon your planet.

The controllers of the inverted matrix system rely now upon those backup generators, yet they are limited in what power they generate and what they can do (see note at end of chapter).

This is a very similar scenario that occurred in the time of Atlantis. This time (your now), you have much more light with which to work. You have much more support from the light levels and from your 'galactic star brothers and sisters'.

The key to immobilisation of the backup generators and black box programmes is moving 'beyond Atlantis' and taking 'lessons from a living Lemuria'.

It is the peaceful, loving, harmonious energies of Lemuria (the crystal gene) when combined with the power, intelligence and technology of the Atlanteans (the indigo flame) that shall give you the key. That key will assist in the transmutation of negative goddess Kali, as the womb expression of Earth, into positive goddess Kali as the divine feminine power expression of 'New Earth' or 'Gaia'.

Note:

Update added on January 13th 2020:

Since the transmission of this material took place, a reboot of the ascension timeline occurred around the time of the Indigo Lunar Eclipse on the 10th of January 2020 and the three days following the eclipse. The reboot was completed on January the 13th (we speak here in linear time). The 'backup generators' we speak of in this transmission, "Lessons from a Living Lemuria", are no longer in place as of the 13th of January 2020. The service-to-self groups now rely only on the recycling of 'old programmes' and cannot generate any new negatively polarised negative eventualities and potentials.

This is explained more fully within the two videos that were uploaded to YouTube at this time.

The videos can be viewed at youtube.com/MagentaPixie2012

See "Indigo Lunar Eclipse, 10th January 2020 (The Paradise Program)" and "11th, 12th and 13th January 2020 - Creation of the Galactic, Diamond Grid"

10: Crystallisation and the Wisdom Codes

Is it not the case that once you reach enlightenment, you can literally eat anything and transmute it? You could even drink poison and it would not harm you?

There is indeed truth to this. When an individual is that which we call 'fully crystalline', the silicate matrices within the body hold so much light they are able to literally turn anything consumed into light.

However, there are caveats to this. A 'fully crystalline' individual is extremely sensitive to the like-vibrational match. This individual is drawn to all things 'fifth dimensional', if you will. Therefore this individual would not hold the desire to consume 'literally anything', neither would the individual desire to consume that which is seen as 'poison'.

This individual, through desire in alignment (as an intentional convergence focus in spiral formation rather than a 'cause and effect' line of intention) would not draw these lower vibrational foodstuffs or that which is poison into their reality.

This fully crystalline individual would eat 'foods of light' which would be plant-based foods, liquids and light itself.

The spiritual teacher, guru or 'ascended master on Earth' may consume these things as part of a teaching tool to present the wisdom codes for others to learn from, but would certainly not be consuming these items as a staple.

If the fully crystalline individual were to consume these lower vibrational foodstuffs for long enough, eventually this would create a denser vibrational state within the body and the individual would begin to descend back to a carbon molecular structure. The transmutation of lower vibrational matter into a crystalline match that is light would not continue indefinitely.

The eating of the lower vibrational food items are one tool into descension from crystalline silicate molecular structure into carbon-based molecular structure.

We might also add that 'fully crystalline' is therefore not a fixed destination. One remains within a harmonising state with the fifth dimensional light of the surrounding environment.

Within the journey from fully carbon to fully crystalline, there are many stages and fluctuations. A crystalline individual within the transmutation between carbon and crystalline enters a highly sensitive state of being. At this stage, one begins to 'live within' the fully crystallised state. The reason for this is that the consciousness one holds creates the manifested match in matter. It is therefore most necessary for the crystallising individual to 'live within' the higher dimensional state. The blueprinted pattern for the future self/higher self/best version of self is downloaded into all the intelligent light fields and portals within the physical being.

That being can then move into a state of 'full belief' (believing they are fully crystalline as in fully ascended, when in truth they are within transmutation towards fully crystalline and are currently within the awakening stages of this).

It is necessary, as we have said, to hold the state of full belief (believing you are fully crystalline) in order to create that as a physical manifestation. Yet without the grounding, understanding and wisdom codes holding knowing of the carbon to crystalline process within (ascension), then one can become 'lost' within the belief structure that is the creation of the physical template and move into extremely ungrounded thinking.

If the individual, within the transitionary state, were to thus continue to consume low vibrational foods (or take poison to prove the point that they can transmute any substance within into light) then this act becomes detrimental to the crystallising/ ascending individual.

Having said all this, crystallising light as a molecular matrix within the body is made of zero-point field plasma. This is a transmutable substance and can thus raise the frequency of anything within the body to the level of that zero-point field. The plasma (as a pure creational substance) makes copies of itself from the foodstuffs, liquids and other substances entering into the body.

What we are saying here is that this is a delicate process, and thus a delicate balance must be created through the wisdom codes activated within the deep cellular structure created by grounding.

When it comes to foodstuffs utilised as a grounding tool then we again draw your attention towards the roots, that which grows underground or very close to the ground. We speak of that which you know as 'starchy vegetables'. The tubers, roots and also the squashes and other vegetables within the squash family such as the pumpkin (which holds a magickal quality in and of itself).

The squashes are not roots per se but hold the same ability to ground.

Of course, grounding is not only achieved through consuming root vegetables. The crystals, rocks and stones hold much benefit as do the anchoring of oneself to the Earth through barefoot walking, standing and certain movements of the physical body.

Ultimately, the mind and the consciousness holds the greatest tool here for grounding, expanding, ascending and crystallising.

The belief is key, yet this must be belief rooted within the wisdom codes so the belief becomes a paradigm. With belief, there is room for doubt as it is a constructing structure in formulation. The paradigm is then a constructed and formed structure, built with a good strong foundation (grounded wisdom codes). There is no room for doubt within the paradigm.

The paradigm holds the convergence geometric presentation of creation which is 'instant karma'/'instant manifestation' zero-point field creation, as opposed to 'cause and effect' (karma).

This is that which we call 'karma-free'. It is simply a raise in construction of the intention. The intention is no longer a birth point/start point (at the beginning of a linear cause and effect process), but the never-ending/always there/zero-point. The intention and the manifestation are simultaneous. This is that which is known upon your planet as the 'lack of desire', the 'end of desire' or the 'transcendence of desire'. Yet in truth, it is none of these things for desire is very much there. It is simply a unification of desire, with the outcome of that desire as a simultaneous manifestation rather than a linear process between desire and outcome.

Carbon-based molecular structure = Linear line of intention. Cause and effect. Karma. Geometric horizontal line. The divine architecture of the matrix construction.

Crystalline/silicon/silicate-based molecular structure = Creation spiral convergence as intention and simultaneous manifestation. Karma-free. Geometric spiralling toroidal field. The transmutation of the divine architecture of the matrix into stargate ascension.

In order to create the correct 'power', 'magnetic/electric charge' or 'force' in order to alchemise from carbon-based into crystalline-based, one needs to generate a substance within the body that we call 'quantum convergence charge' or 'blue starphire'.

This is a shift from a dormant plasma structure into an activated and transmuted plasmic light structure. The 'blue starphire' needs an energetic pattern in order to be created. This energetic pattern is the liquid plasma and plasma light. It is known by many names upon your planet such as 'qhi', 'chi' or 'life force'. It is also in a more physicalised sense known as 'manna', 'white powder gold' or 'ormus'. It is created within the body as the carbon dormant plasma 'wakes up' (the great awakening) and transmutes into the activated plasmic light.

Whilst this is created through mind/consciousness/paradigm, it is a magnetic attracting force drawing to itself the like-vibrational structures within the physical reality. Within this magnetic attraction of physical reality, there are many 'substances' (as well as people, events, places, situations, ideas, emotions and so on). One of these substances is the foodstuffs you consume for nourishment.

The foodstuffs holding the like-vibration will be 'ormus-filled'/'light-filled'. The transmutation to create that ormus/ light comes from your physical sun. It also comes from the grand cosmic suns or central suns of which your physical sun (the intelligent and loving being 'Sol') is an emanation of.

The ormus/sunlight-filled foodstuffs are that which are living, raw and plant-based. Thus here you shall find your blue starphire. That which you need to create the alchemisation from carbon-based to crystalline, silicate, phire-matrix. (Your light body or fifth/sixth dimensional Mer-Ka-Bah vehicles.)

So what are 'wisdom codes'?

These are simply memory codes. They are that which present to you the true knowing of the human template, the human journey and the transmutation from carbon to crystalline that we speak of. This is known to you as 'innate wisdom' that is simply activated cellular memory. When you hold this cellular memory in its activated state, you hold wisdom. This is perceived by you as 'knowing' (one may refer to this as 'clairsentience' for it is a perception of reality through the 'sixth sense') and also as 'wisdom'. You will hold wisdom, present wisdom and 'be most wise' if you will. You are thus the spiritual teacher, master or guru. However, you are still but an innocent once you achieve the activation of these wisdom codes for there is more upon your ascension journey, so much more.

Yet it is here that the 'fun starts' if you will. The enjoyment (contentment, happiness, joy, bliss) of life is thus experienced once this state is achieved. You shall 'shine with your creativity' and those wisdom codes are delivered to all those who interact with you.

You do what we call 'radiate'. This is service-to-others, positive polarisation. It is the opposite of 'absorption' which is the service-to-self, negative polarisation.

Once you begin to 'radiate' en masse then your entire planet, timeline and dimension shifts into the like-vibration of that which you create. Plasmic light begets plasmic light (remember we are looking here at a cosmic photocopying organic action).

As the blue starphire is accessed through the raw plant foods, you can thus see what an intrinsically important subject 'nutrition' is! Coupled with the understanding of 'karma' and the moving into the 'karma-free' state, one can see why we present this transmission through the seed points of these two highly significant subjects.

You spoke of transmutation of liquid light and the release of traumas within the womb for the women. How do the males transmute the energy they receive during the sexual act? How does this affect homosexual couples?

Males do not receive energy, they are givers of energy. The male does not need to transmute anything they 'hold on to' if you will. Their journey of integration is specific to where they place their energy. There must be trust between the male and female.

If the male gives his precious seed, full of life force, that which we call 'liquid light', then that is part of him. It contains his genetic and etheric blueprint (all that he is). This can be utilised by the female who receives and holds the energy. It can be used for both creation and destruction. The male creates a bond or telepathic link with every female he gives his liquid light to. So he needs to be in a place of trust with that female, knowing that she will hold that liquid light and utilise it as the divine creatrix that she is and not move into the manipulation and control tactics of negative Kali.

If a child is wished for by the couple then it is just as important for the male to be in a healthy state as it is the female. This ensures the liquid light substance is in the healthiest and most aligned state possible. However, even if a child is not wished for by the couple but together they are in a creator/creatrix union, then it is equally as important to create healthy and high vibrational liquid light. This will be utilised by the female to catalyse the Kundalini and DNA activation into the creation of 'quantum convergence charge' or 'blue starphire' for stargate ascension. This then 'feeds back' to the male partner as they continue to exchange energy through their ongoing physical relationship.

Therefore the male's focus here is not transmutation and release of sexual energy but *where he places his focus.* The woman does not need to create an intention as a creational outcome of the sexual act within the sexual union. It is the male that creates that intention. So he holds that intentional line of focus within his mind and heart before, during or after (or all three) as a manifestation or creational outcome for the couple.

The female can do this also, especially if she has a strong, activated, sacred masculine energy through the indigo aspect of self, yet there is no need for her to do this when they work together with tantric sex magick.

The male is directional and stands as the vertical and horizontal axis of the matrix within his energy blueprint. This matches the biological presentation he holds and the movement created within the sexual act itself.

The female is holistic, spiralling and circular. She stands as the zero-point/pivot point/central point (the time nexus) and the event horizon of the matrix within her energy blueprint. (See *The Infinite Helix and the Emerald Flame* for more information on the matrix formation and the event horizon.) This matches the biological presentation she holds and the movement created within the sexual act itself.

It is important (crucial for planetary ascension) for the heterosexual males and heterosexual females to be fully rooted and fully anchored within their biology and energy fields. It is equally as important to be in a state of complete acceptance of all other expressions of gender (gender-neutral, transgender, homosexual and so on) whilst at the same time not losing the focus of their own individual identity. The black box programme regarding gender confusion seeks to take away the individualised and anchored heterosexual identity, whilst at the same time marginalising and creating prejudices against individuals who hold a gender or identity outside of the 'male/female norms'.

It is important for those who embrace a particular gender identity to stand strong and anchored within it. At the same time it is equally as important for the fluidity of gender expression to be allowed to flourish without limits in that specific sense for an individual who chooses to reject gender for themselves and stand as gender-fluid or neutral.

As one stands strong within their own individual expression, one creates a harmonious society. One cannot reject gender itself on a societal level. These belief systems and agendas are part of the black box programme hijacking we speak of. They exist within third and fourth dimensional constructs. Once you embrace the fifth dimensional bandwidth, you 'transcend' this black box hijacking and integrate the anchoring we speak of.

The 'higher' you go, the more rooted you are within your individuality and your expression on all levels. This applies to homosexual individuals and those who hold different gender identities to their biological forms.

Regarding transmutation of homosexual couples. With two males who are fully rooted within their gender expression as males but who are homosexual, you have predominantly 'givers' of energy. However, there is a certain fluidity within the individual relationship itself and many of these stand as twin flame couples. Therefore we would say to the homosexual couple who are both incarnated males, that whilst transmutation of holding energy is not needed in the same way as the biological female (as in release of that which is held), we would still recommend a transmutation and a focused intention for the sexual act.

If this sexual act is outside of true love and a true twin flame union, then a destructive energy can be created, feeding lesser fourth dimensional life forms. If the couple hold unconditional love between them and live expressing the twin flame union, then this moves into the true divine marriage and is no different within the creative ability of the heterosexual couple.

The blue starphire is created, the liquid light is given and received, Kundalini is activated, DNA is reconstructed and stargate ascension takes place. The energy here is unconditional love, it is always love. The kindness, compassion and open-hearted energy is the focus, regardless of sexual orientation or gender expression.

With the homosexual female couple, you have predominantly receivers of energy. Again, there are nuances that can be created through the unique pattern of the relationship. We would suggest that the homosexual females move through the transmutation processes just like heterosexual females. They still hold the receptacle and the goddess Kali can manifest in her negative or positive forms.

The focus again is unconditional love. The twin flame and divine marriage union takes place between the homosexual females and they are as much creatrix goddesses as the heterosexual females are.

These presentations are basic and somewhat stereotypical. The nuances and flavours within each individual, and within each unique relationship, present in a myriad of formations.

Remember, the relationship itself is an intelligent, living consciousness with a developing identity of its own. No two individuals are alike (even identical biological incarnated twins) and therefore no two relationships are alike.

Many homosexual relationships move into patterns of masculine and feminine. However, it is a fallacy that one partner 'takes on' the male aspect and the other the 'female' aspect. They can both be fully male, fully female or combinations of both. As we have said, the presentations are unique and individual. The point here being that transmutation may have to take place, just as in the case with the heterosexual female. The focused intentions for the creation and manifestation of the sexual act would also take place. The homosexual twin flame relationships, when love and balance are in place, present as the fully-formed matrix with vertical, horizontal and circular/spiralling energies morphing into place for stargate or accelerated ascension.

We have spoken regarding the female integration and transmutation of held energy and we provide an aligned meditation, 'The Golden Chalice', at the end of this transmission.

The male transmutation of traumas and energies (and sexual abuse takes place in various ways within males also) would be undertaken in the same methods we listed within this transmission previously. We spoke of such things as yoga, massage, crystal work and also the importance of following the high vibrational diet. However, we may also add that the martial arts path is most in alignment for the incarnated male. The martial arts path can act as a powerful transmutation of energy and healing tool. This path can also be very effective for the female, most especially indigo females. The indigo is the male energy and the crystal is the female energy.

It is far more helpful, if you have any resistance to a gender or sexual expression that is outside your own, to think of individuals in terms of their energy such as indigo, crystal, blue ray, rose ray and so on. This puts you back into a state of unity as you see not 'that which is opposing to you' or 'outside of you' but that which unifies *with you* as part of the rainbow. It is no coincidence that the LGBT communities use the rainbow as their emblem. However, this is a third dimensional interpretation for the 'true rainbow' encompasses every individual and indeed those beyond your planet.

It is also helpful to be fully aware of the fact that gender identity, gender expression, sexuality and sexual expression are all different templates. Sometimes they merge and interject and in many cases (within rooted heterosexuality) they unify completely. In other cases, they remain separate.

It is the divine right of the individual, through free will and choice, to express themselves however they choose to, without prejudice or fear of being ostracised from society. These 'boundaries' are to be anchored within the individual to create the unification that is the rainbow and for the individual to take their place as a rainbow warrior.

These templates rooted within the divine right and free will of the individual are not to cross over into society at large. As in, *you cannot force a paradigm you hold upon a demographic* for this shall create resistance and thus division, the opposite of unification. This is the agenda for these various black box programmes. The antidote in these cases is the 'rainbow warrior template'.

The rainbow warrior template is one of unification. This is the template that reconstructs and heals the destruction that has occurred through black box programmes and inverted matrix manipulation.

Eating the rainbow diet plan assists you to come into that rainbow within on an energetic level, not just individually but collectively.

Do you see how all things are connected? This puts a whole new perspective upon the phrase, "You are what you eat."

A shift or change at the local (or individual) level affects the global (cosmic) level. A shift or change at the global level affects the local level. As above, so below.

This is the macrocosmic and the microcosmic realities in unification (in reaction to each other - karma, if you will).

Eating a fully (or predominantly) plant-based diet creates peace individually. The more individuals that consume plant foods, the more peace is created at the global level.

Eating factory farmed animals creates fear, chaos and conflict individually. So the more people that eat factory farmed animal products, the more fear, conflict and chaos is created at the global level. This is the purpose behind the hijacking (ultimately preventing ascension).

Yet the plant-based movement can also be hijacked by the mass creation of 'Frankenfoods', as in highly processed foodstuffs.

Hence we present to you the 'whole foods plant-based' lifestyle that is the Lemurian way.

If you are rooted within your identity and hold self-love and love within the relationship with and for your partner, then you cannot be hijacked or infiltrated. The rooting is the grounding or anchoring into the unification of individualisation.

Yet becoming anchored within your gender identity is a journey and there are those who have not yet anchored or rooted themselves. If you are looking to do this, then consuming the root vegetables will assist you greatly for they are the 'roots' you are looking for. As above, so below.

There are those who choose not to anchor or root themselves. Through free will and choice, this is their divine right.

When you are anchored and rooted within who you are, then you move into an alchemised state, that which we call 'alchemical unification'. We shall present more specific work on alchemical unification in future transmissions. Know that, in response to your quest, it matters not if the couple are heterosexual, homosexual, a merge of such or alternate between. The gender expression matters not. The sexual expression as monogamy or polygamy matters not. What is the issue is your integrity, your honour, your sovereignty and your anchored and focused intention through alchemical unification. One needs to ask oneself if one can keep that integrity and sovereignty within the lifestyle they have chosen to embrace and experience.

When you stand in integrity and sovereignty, you thus take your part within that rainbow as a 'rainbow warrior' or indeed a balanced and unconditionally loving crystallised system of light.

Let us now in turn move through each of the foodstuffs that would replicate the original Lemurian diet.

Fruits

The fruits, when grown naturally in rich soil, with love, present to you the greatest amount of blue starphire. Yet these must be eaten in abundance in order to create the blue starphire in its correct formation within. Each fruit item holds a slightly different configuration that shall work uniquely within your bodies to cultivate the balance you are looking for. The blue starphire is found predominantly within the juices or waters of the fruit. Yet one needs to consume the flesh, seeds and skins of the fruit (in most cases) in order for the juices and the waters to assimilate in correct flow within your physical bodies. These fruits are that which we call 'cleansing' or 'detoxifying' for they hold a purification element. This purification element is so essential for your ascension and crystallisation for it assists you in the release of toxins and traumas on all levels.

There are many dietary teachers upon your planet that will present to you that you should restrict the fruits within your nutritional plans. This is based upon the sugar/carbohydrate/fructose element of the fruit and how it may relate to the insulin within your bodies. There is truth to this only when the fruits are consumed in combination with other, more heavier foodstuffs. Yet even combining fruits with other foods rarely affects the ascending/crystallising individual. These dietary teachers work with third dimensional information only and are not aware of the blue starphire or of the differences between physical body requirements and light body requirements. Having said this, there are indeed 'spiritual masters' on your planet teaching nutritional requirements for both physical body and light body. We suggest you seek these masters out if you wish to study this subject in depth, as we touch only on the basics within this transmission which is specific to karma and karma-free states rather than light body nutrition per se.

The fruits hold the keycodes and the information/messages within their juices and waters. The ascending, crystallising individual is advised to consume these fruits in their raw state in abundance and hold these as dietary staples as you move through the ascension process.

There is one fruit that is more nourishing than cleansing and holds a very high level of blue starphire, assisting greatly with the charge needed for stargate ascension. We speak of the avocado. We recommend these are consumed regularly within ascending and crystallising individuals.

Vegetables

These foodstuffs make up the nourishing element of your dietary plan. They also hold keycodes, information and messages most especially when consumed in their raw state. The lightly cooked or heated vegetables hold value also, yet we would suggest that much is consumed in the raw and original state. These items provide that which nourishes and supports the physical body and builds the physical body. This creates a foundation for the fruits to 'do their work' and to cleanse and detoxify the physical body as they construct the light body/crystalline body.

One can see the fruits as the feminine/antimatter/light aspect of the overall nutritional plan and the vegetables as the masculine/ matter/physical aspect. These were known in Lemurian culture as 'moonlight foods' (feminine) and 'sunlight foods' (masculine). This Lemurian knowledge has been preserved and handed down somewhat through indigenous cultures living harmoniously upon your planet.

It is therefore true to say that, in most cases, the incarnated physical female will require more fruits and the incarnated physical male will require more vegetables.

However, this is a generalisation as many of you stand 'outside the box' when it comes to gender identity, gender expression and gender presentation. We would say to you that if you present as female then you will require more fruits regardless of biological gender (hence the reason why so many who fluctuate with gender identity are attracted to the sugars, as they hold a higher requirement for glucose).

The vegetables are to be consumed also in abundance and bring forward the masculine aspect that is 'strength'. They therefore create the strength within the body. If you are aiming to build physical strength and stamina within your body (we speak not of the act that you know as 'body building', just simply the requirement for a strong, balanced physical body able to cope with the demands that third dimensional living can present) then the vegetables, most especially the dark green vegetables, will be that which you will require.

The substance that builds the strength within the body comes from the being that nurtures your planetary Earth, your physical sun, the being known as 'Sol'. Your Sol is a male entity so therefore the consuming of the light codes from Sol present as a masculine aspect. This is the strength not only of body, but of mind. If you are looking for empowerment, assertiveness, courage and confidence, then the vegetables, most especially the dark green leafy vegetables, will give you this. The energy of Sol is held in abundance within the substance you know as 'chlorophyll'. This substance is, when seen through your physical light spectrum, a neon yellow (the exact colour of the solar plexus chakra - your power centre). The colour looks to your eyes as green (the colour of your heart chakra) due to the way the light reflects upon your planet.

The solar plexus and the heart are your anchoring points. These are the chakras within your energy matrix that stand as the zero-point, pivot point, nexus point of the entire matrix that is all that is you. These are the central points from which all things radiate. The physical body is a direct replica match of the energetic body. The heart and the stomach (gut) are the centres holding the interfaces that decode reality. The heart is the centre for the knowing through compassion and the stomach/gut is the centre for knowing through power. Both are centres for your intuition.

They are physical processing centres for your connection to the pillar of light, vertical axis of the matrix.

Within your physical bodies, these points act like mini-brains (when activated and in balance). The brain processes the third dimensional reality, the heart processes the higher/heaven realm/positive vibrations (through emotion) and the gut processes the lower/hell dimension/negative (also through emotion). One could call this the 'God/Lucifer alignment'.

When we use terms such as 'hell' and 'Lucifer', these are not meant to create in you a fear reaction. These words and that which they emote and invoke are hijacked by service-to-self factions upon your planet. Hell/Lucifer/negative/below is simply the polarisation to heaven/God/positive/above. They are simply opposite directions or frequencies.

This is depicted within your divination expression known as the 'tarot'. The reversals in tarot are often seen as negative, but in truth they are 'that which is subconscious' rather than negative or bad. The reason the reversals are seen as negative is because the average third dimensional individual with any trauma-based experiences and fears often suppresses them within their subconscious. Yet once the traumas begin to clear and release and you create immunity from the hijacking upon your planet (see material in *Masters of the Matrix*) then the subconscious simply holds 'that which is unprocessed' or 'that which the conscious aspect is not yet fully aware of' and is awaiting integration. The subconscious is that which we explored previously within this transmission when presenting the energetics you know as 'the womb'. This is not a positive/negative polarity in the context of good or bad.

The polarisation upon your planet has been held down in such strong polarity through hijacking of the negative polarity. Hijacking of that 'moonlight energy' or subconscious, distorting it into something bad or evil. In the highest truth, this polarity of positive/negative is simply matter and antimatter. The merge of both creates the enlightenment or ascension through trinity awareness or trilocational consciousness. Hijacking one of these polarities prevents the accessing of the Tao, middle way, rose gold flame or trinity aspect. That which has been hijacked is the true negative polarity (antimatter, moonlight, feminine). The rise of the divine feminine upon your planet puts the negative polarity back in its correct, original and organic placement within the structure of your planetary and thus galactic architecture. This creates the 'lessening of polarity', that you thus experience as a collective humanity.

In order to raise to the crystalline frequency, one needs the positive and negative charge within, in balance in order to create the trinity which is quantum convergence charge or blue starphire. Therefore we suggest you look at these terminologies simply as 'yin' and 'yang'. That which gives you balance and neither one is 'good or bad'. They are simply right and left, night and day or sun and moon.

The vegetables, most especially the dark green vegetables containing the chlorophyll, assist you and give to you this yin/yang balance for they hold this balance in perfect combination within their stems, leaves and shoots.

We may also mention the mushrooms and fungi. These are highly intelligent plants and many are starseeds like you (seeded from the stars) or we could say they are 'extraterrestrial' as many originated outside of your Earth and were 'brought to your planet'. There are within these fungi foods both the edible and the inedible. Within those edible, one finds the neon luminescent seeds for the glowing gemstone keycodes within DNA activation. These contain the blue starphire even when cooked.

Sea Vegetables

These hold messages and information within. They present in the form of minerals and natural sodiums. In fact, these are mineral-rich although not all sea vegetables are suitable for human consumption. You may be surprised to know that many sea vegetables have not yet been discovered upon your planet and remain within the depths of the unexplored ocean regions. Yet other sea vegetables, abundant in life-giving force, have been discovered by the very few naturally living indigenous peoples and are not yet presented to humanity on a larger scale.

However, there are many edible sea vegetables available on a larger scale to humanity that one can consume. Look for those from clean and clear waters. The sea vegetables pair extremely well with crystals for cleansing, so they can be soaked in crystal water before consumption if you wish.

These foodstuffs are highly 'intelligent', if you will. They hold a higher awareness of existence than the land grown vegetables, they connect you with the mind through the detoxification of the body and pineal gland. They are both cleansing and nourishing simultaneously and are both masculine and feminine simultaneously. Many connect you into 'extraterrestrial' awareness (many were brought to your planet, yet others were natively grown within your seas).

For the one who is fully plant-based, holding a vegan philosophy, then the sea vegetables will give to you the same fourth dimensional connection one would receive from the consuming of seafoods such as fish. We highly recommend the consumption of the mineral-rich sea vegetables. Often the ascending/crystallising individual is led to sea vegetables through synchronicity and magick.

Coconut

Whilst the flesh, cream and oils made from the coconut hold much benefit, the coconut milk is of special import. When we say 'milk', we speak here of the natural electrolyte fluids that one can consume direct from the live coconut. However, many of the properties of this natural milk is carried forward into sustainably created coconut milks and creams.

The liquid within the coconut holds a very high charge and is almost one hundred percent blue starphire. This is a 'conducting charge'. It acts as a 'fuse to light the fire', if you will. Whilst this holds cleansing and nourishing properties, it is best explained as having 'conducting' properties. It holds 'pure life force', if you will. The coconut water/milk/cream is therefore most advised for the ascending/crystallising individual and was eaten heartily amongst the Lemurians (their coconuts were different from yours of your today moment but there is much similarity).

The conducting capacity, whilst most abundant in the raw milk found inside the coconut, translates to all naturally created coconut products. Even coconut products heated and changed still hold some of the original conducting charge, such is the power of the original and raw coconut. Visionary states can be achieved through the consumption of the highly charged raw milk. This food item is therefore most beneficial for the ascending soul.

Nuts and Seeds

In order for these to be valuable to the ascending individual, they must be consumed raw. The heated or roasted nuts, whilst still holding some nourishment for the physical body, hold also a change that is potentially detrimental.

The raw nuts are extremely nourishing and just a few provide a meal in themselves. One does not need to consume a high number of nuts to access their benefits. In their raw state, they hold messages and information. A few, eaten alongside the green vegetables, assist with the creation of blue starphire within the body. Having said this, there are starseeds who do not align with nuts and they would be toxic to that particular starseed. They are not a foodstuff that is appropriate for all. They do have value and provide a bridge for the plant-based ascending individuals to obtain dense nourishment easily. Eating a few in number can assist in the creation of blue starphire, for you only need a few to create charge. Yet if too many are eaten, this can create an opposite effect of sluggishness rather than charge. Yet this effect would be temporary as the crystallising individual transmutes this effect rapidly.

Some seeds hold a high level of charge creation, more so than the nuts and similar to the coconut milk. Whilst not one hundred percent blue starphire as with the coconut, there are seeds that hold an abundance of this. Most especially the chia and the linseed (flax). However, there are many seeds upon your planet that are toxic to humans and other life.

This information is widely available from the dietary teachers and masters upon your planet and we would advise you to use the conscious intuition that you naturally hold within as an ascending starseed. The intuitive abilities and higher connection you have will guide you, through synchronicity, to the master who is in alignment with these teachings or shall draw down the downloads from your own higher self, or both.

Root Vegetables

We have spoken of the root vegetables and their grounding influence. These are nourishing foods and can be eaten as a staple alongside the vegetables and fruits. The root vegetables have a 'magickal' property to them just as the squash you know as 'pumpkin' also holds.

Root vegetables are discovered underground. They grow within the darkness, the shadow. They are buried until ripe to eat.

These root vegetables, when consumed in their whole form (as close to their natural origin as possible although some root vegetables will be cooked or heated in order to make them edible) trigger within the secrets, the dark and the shadow. They 'draw up' the buried traumas and the subconscious belief systems operating in the background. The magickal quality we speak of is their ability to 'draw out of the shadow, that which needs to be presented to the light'. This can be, of course, both positive and negative for the one who consumes them. This depends on the level of buried traumas as opposed to 'mysteries' within the subconscious. They are, of course, often intertwined. Even in the trauma, the negative, there are gifts.

We mean 'positive' and 'negative' in this sense to mean obviously beneficial or obviously detrimental. We say 'obviously' because even that which is detrimental is of benefit in a wholistic sense, which is what we mean when we say 'gifts'!

The pumpkin holds magickal energy due to the fact that its symbolism sits within the collective consciousness of humanity as an alphabetical numeral (or fire letter). It has the ability to trigger subconscious awareness and knowing of the 'darkness' or 'shadow' within humanity as a whole. This also extends to 'that which is hidden', therefore the pumpkin and the root vegetables shall 'lead you to truth' if you consume them. When you consume them with intention and awareness, then this works 'doubly strong'.

The pumpkin as a symbol of magick within your Western societies at the time of Samhain, known to many as 'Halloween', stands ever stronger within the language of light. This has been strengthened through its use in children's fairy tales upon your planet.

However, the pumpkin's magickal reverence goes back even further. The reason for its perception as such a magickal foodstuff goes back to Celtic tribal folklore and superstitions of that time, occurring through synchronicity. Many of those starseeded individuals known as 'white witches' used pumpkins within their magickal spellcasting.

The pumpkin, along with all squashes, holds much blue starphire and the codes for the charge translate over even when these are heated and cooked.

Beans

In order for the beans to be edible for human consumption, they must be cooked or sprouted. Cooking the beans creates the nourishing element that provides a most 'in alignment' array of rainbow nutrients to support the physical body of the ascending starseed. Small amounts of blue starphire remain within the bean even after cooking. However, the nutrients within the bean assist the physical body in the creation of its own blue starphire within. The sprouting of the beans (and we mean other pulses also) create very high amounts of blue starphire, for the sprouts are young, living shoots. Not all beans and pulses are appropriate for sprouting however, and can be toxic to the human. So seek out the masters of nutrition upon your planet for the teachings. There are many variables within your natural land and that which grows within the garden that is Earth. It is beyond the scope of this transmission to present in depth the edible and the inedible.

Herbs

The teaching here is vast so allow yourself to move into the zero-point state of awareness that shall draw to you, through synchronicity and magick, the information you need regarding the herbs. We include here the wildly growing plants and nettles. These are your 'nature's medicines' and when there is imbalance within the physical body or a need for acceleration within light body activation then the herbal kingdom shall contain the remedy or tool.

There is much within this herbal kingdom containing blue starphire or the seeds for blue starphire activation. Yet so too are there such that can prevent blue starphire activation and dim your light. The masters that teach the informations regarding the herbal kingdom are plentiful and your synchronistic, magickal workings shall draw them or their creations into your life. You have but to ask (with a pure heart) for this information.

The herbs contain an abundance of light codes and messages, and ascending starseeds are most in alignment with the particular gifts and knowledge they have to impart. These plants are actually, in and of themselves, 'plant teachers'. The consuming of them (raw or even as a lightly brewed tea) awaken within the sensitive ones the information contained within. These information codes present as a 'living library', meaning they come forward in real time.

We refer you to the chapter of the *Divine Architecture and the Starseed Template* transmission entitled the 'The Superhero Program' in order for explanation as to how the teachings of this living plant library works.[5]

_____

5   "Divine Architecture and the Starseed Template" (2017) by Magenta Pixie

12: Living Lemuria and the Mushroom Masters

Why do you say 'living Lemuria'? What do you mean by this?

Lemuria is, as we have said, a time period within your planetary history. The memories of Lemuria are 'embedded' or 'written' into the 'software' of all that is you, programmed into your DNA.

Yet your knowings, thoughts, beliefs and paradigms, when cohesive, create reality. As each of you access these memories and begin to 'remember' Lemuria, you bring Lemuria itself online. As you also do with Atlantis.

Within the true reality, there is no time, as in a linear sense. The future, present and past do not sit upon a continuum but are one moment. One convergence point (zero-point). Lemuria and Atlantis thus exist from this perspective.

The 'you' that you 'were' (or are, or will be) that lives within the Lemurian times can be communicated with and indeed merged with.

Lemuria existed 'before' the fall. There was no 'before' because that higher dimensional reality fabric was not expressed linearly. Lemuria is therefore a never-ending reality. It is infinite (infinite paradise or immortal bliss).

There has never been, in your history of your planet Earth, a better time to connect with your Lemurian self than right now. Why is this? The reason for this is because you are 'going back' (or going forward, depending on perspective) to the higher dimensional reality fabric, and thus the zero-point experience. Your reality will be much like Lemuria with the cohesive experience garnered and gathered through the many soul incarnations you have had since.

The reason why we refer to Lemuria as 'living' is because of this current now moment existence that it holds. It is not 'that which once was', it exists for you now. The 'place' where Lemuria (and

Atlantis) exist (on a physical, geological level) is not at this moment tangible. There are many who search for land, rock, tree, sea and sand. Yet Lemuria does not present as physical at the nexus point that is your today moment. Both Lemuria and Atlantis are therefore antimatter and non-physical (and fifth dimensional).

Yet you are anchoring this time period all the time as you recover these memories. As you begin to remember, you construct a reality that matches those memories. This makes Lemuria a living society, a living structure with living Lemurian beings you can connect with.

Even if you do not have 'memories' of Lemuria or living in Lemurian times, we can assure you that you are indeed of Lemurian descent on a soul level if you are a starseed. Once you activate the 'starseed template code', which is the awakening of cellular memory and the reconstruction of the organic DNA configuration, you awaken and 'activate that software'. It is hardwired into the diamond codex memory fields of all who reach that which we call 'the fifth strand'. This would apply to each and every starseed.

This is why you have knowing regarding your connection to Lemuria. It is not that you are looking at a 'past life' per se (although it is that). You are actually experiencing planetary memory grids, that you are each connected to. The planetary memory becomes your memory. The planetary mind becomes your mind. Not only will you hold the perspective of living and existing within Lemuria, you will also hold the memory of *creating* Lemuria. You are, indeed, the planetary architect once you hold planetary memory.

This is fifth strand awakening. Then you move into galactic memory and hold the perspective of the galactic being, your inception seed point of Pleiadian, Sirian or Lyran. Indeed, you then hold the perspective of being the architect of the galaxy or of the universe.

Within Atlantis, the memories are somewhat different as Atlantis occurred *after* the fall. They had 'technologies' however, and a fully functioning crystalline planetary and galactic grid structure with a 'full set', if you will, of planetary and galactic stargates. What this means for you within your linear time period is that every starseed, whilst intrinsically connected to the Atlantean memory, did not necessarily have Atlantean incarnations. Yet each one of you lived as a Lemurian being. You each hold the Lemurian template.

When you balance Lemuria and Atlantis within, as we have said, you combine or merge the crystal self with the indigo self, or the feminine with the masculine. As you do this, you recreate the original Lemurian grid system and all its patterning which is that of the planet you know as Gaia rather than Earth. As *children of Gaia*, which indeed you are, you are also *children of Lemuria.*

Lemuria lives on in each of you, in your deep cellular memory and in your hearts. The society was beautiful beyond your imaginings, the Lemurian beings were much beloved and revered throughout your solar system and universe. This is now becoming the way for all the awakened starseeds at fifth strand level. You are so very much beloved and revered, for you radiate a rainbow gemstone glow into the etheric layers of reality as your mind twinkles with knowing. Your realisations create shooting stars into the etheric, and your heart glow is seen for miles in space and millennia in time as you anchor compassion and joy and create within you passion. Passion for life and for all and everything that holds life and is living.

The foods within your plant and herbal kingdom contain the Lemurian codes and the Lemurian memories. They glow with the neon crystallisation of a plant flooded with blue starphire.

The mushrooms, as we have spoken about, hold the codes for this neon brilliance or luminescent glow within, as do many of the algaes.

The Doctrine of Signatures

In ancient Lemuria, one of the 'laws of the land' is that which you would know as 'magic'. Yet for others, you may call this science.

In truth, this was simply an acknowledged and known harmony betwixt the Lemurian peoples and their environments.

The environment would literally 'form itself' to the consciousness of the peoples. The people would learn from the environment and thus access knowledge and form ideas, creations, health, wisdom and strength.

The environment and the peoples were literally one. This is known throughout the galactic, cosmic multiverse as the 'Law of One'.

This tangible evidence of the Law of One in action is returning to your planet and your peoples. That which we present as a harmonious interaction and merge with one's environment.

In ancient Lemuria, one of the ways this Law of One, harmonious interaction would present itself was from plants and roots, seeds and fruits that would literally grow in response to the collective consciousness of the peoples. Foodstuffs grown in the natural world began to resemble the parts of the human body or energy system that would bring healing and balance to that human organism. This is known in your teachings today as 'the doctrine of signatures' and also within that which you know as 'the law of similars'. The understanding of this is the cornerstone of true naturopathic and homeopathic medicine, including herbal and flower infusion remedies that are presented by the master healers upon your planet today.

Much is shrouded in mystery and is a challenge to access for the everyday individual as it is overshadowed by and buried under the presentations of your modern nutrition in the form of processed, denatured, genetically modified and lab created items that resemble foodstuffs but are not indeed true foodstuffs at all.

When you walk in alignment as a 'master on Earth' or that which we call the 'dreamweaver', you merge yourself with the true intelligence of your environment. You begin to live according to the Law of One and you draw these true natural medicines into your life. Your environment begins to literally 'grow itself' for you.

I notice that you have not mentioned grains at all in your template of Lemurian nutrition and that which is most in alignment with an ascending individual. Should we stop eating grains or are they OK to eat?

We attempt to assist you in recreating the 'Garden of Eden' Lemurian nutritional plan that kept them healthy, strong and disease-free. Grain is a difficult one to reproduce as they did not actually eat grains in these times. However, they did create a type of flour or fine flour-like substance made from crushed and dried leaves, fruit and seeds.

Some of the grains you have access to in your modern now times are in fact seeds. These are quite similar in their composition to the Lemurian seeds that were consumed. With a grain-like seed or what is known to you as a 'pseudo grain', then what you are looking for is a blend of the natural healthy fats packed alongside polysaccharide molecular foodstuffs. You know these as 'complex carbohydrates' or 'starches', but in fact it is polysaccharides that the body makes use of in their complete and whole form as close as you would find them in nature. Many hold substances within that are a challenge for the human digestive system so they must be prepared in ways that soften the harsh substances and activate the proliferation of the important polysaccharides. This is done through softening techniques such as long and slow cooking, soaking and other cooking methods. Look to your ancient teachings of how to prepare these foodstuffs as they have indeed been consumed on your planet for many years. These ancient pseudo grains, when prepared in these ways, offer benefit and healing.

The way the modern grains are grown and prepared is not in alignment with the ascending individual who is looking to create light within through consuming light. The modern grains are devoid of this light and no longer contain life. The human organism does not digest these grains and they do not align with the balanced ecosystem within the intestinal micro-worlds within the human.

There is one caveat to this, however, when it comes to that which you call a 'grain'. We speak here of the cereal grain you call 'oat' and the creation of that which you call 'oatmeal' or 'porridge'.

For some of you, this particular grain, the oat, is not in alignment with your system and this and all grains and pseudo grains are best avoided for you. Yet there are those of you descended from the Celtic tribal peoples that lived for many years in your Scottish Highlands and Irish towns. These Celtic individuals (predominantly genetically related to Pleiadian civilisations) were very much at one with their environment and lived in these times in accordance with the Law of One. The abundant plants growing at this time were today that which you may call 'old-fashioned oats', yet that which we speak of are wild grown. The nutrient levels can be recreated in some cases by sprouting these oats, but ultimately we refer to wild grown oats and not cultivated oats. These oats contain a most magikal substance that we have spoken much of to our conduit. This substance is that which you know as the 'beta-glucan'. If these wild oats are tolerated by you well, then you will have retained that which we call the 'Celtic gene'.

These Celtic peoples, through a unique evolutionary process, created a genetic trait within that allowed them to easily digest the wild oats and benefit from the magical beta-glucans within. These beta-glucans literally 'line the stomach'. You will have heard the phrase that oatmeal or porridge (or 'parritch' as it was once called) 'sticks to your ribs'. Whilst indeed it is not the ribs that the oatmeal sticks to, it does create a 'lining' or a 'container' within the stomach and oesophagus that assists with the creation of the balanced ecosystem and the digestion. This thus affects all body systems within their complementary workings. Repair within the stomach lining takes place and other foodstuffs are digested easier when oatmeal is eaten as the first meal of the day. It is not just one meal of oatmeal that creates this but a repeated consuming of this meal on an almost daily basis. This only occurs within the individual who holds the Celtic gene and their genetic line can be traced back to the Scottish or Irish Celts (and prior to that, the Pleiadian civilisations from a linear perspective).

You may think that the Celtic indigenous peoples were only a small number of peoples and whilst this is true, their descendants have spread far and wide, many existing within the Americas now. Your gene testing may show that you hold this ancestry but not all genetic markers show up in your testing. Meditation and alignment with the knowing of who you are will show you if you have this Celtic ancestry. If you do, then consuming the oatmeal or porridge will be of benefit to you. If you do not have this inherited genetic trait, then the consuming of the oatmeal may be best avoided for you along with other grains and pseudo grains. You can see how you are each so different and unique in your make-up and why we say that conscious eating is the way forward for each and every one of you.

You spoke about mushrooms being starseeds and that they were brought to this planet. Is this all mushrooms and fungi? Who brought them here?

One could say the mushrooms were brought to your planet in huge ships that were created for scientific observation. Large gardens were upon these ships and the mushrooms were cultivated from spores from their home planets. The star visitors or extraterrestrials brought these mushrooms to your planet. This would be true. The memory templates created by third dimensional interpretation create the existence of such ships. It is also true to say that the consciousness of this star visitor vessel and all the extraterrestrials on board are triggering your memories through their presence.

However, everything is metaphor for something else. One can always go deeper into the metaphor and unravel its next stage, yet knowing that each stage exists in its own right. This is the fractalisation of the universal and cosmic structure. If you 'dig deep' enough within this metaphoric unfoldment within the fractal, you will discover Source.

So the next level to this metaphor is that these 'mushroom spores' are living consciousness structures. Dimensionally, one could say their origin is the sixth dimension. They are the direct response to music. Certain 'musical notes' within the seventh dimension creates a matching geometric frequency within the sixth dimension. This then formulates as a blueprint and the matter is created from that sixth dimensional blueprint. The original seventh dimensional music remains within the created structure as an energy imprint. If this imprinted signature can be preserved, then the substance or creation holding the imprint can thus pass that imprint to others. One of the resulting creations of this geometric blueprint created in response to these seventh dimensional musical notes are mushroom spores. The other resulting creations of these geometric blueprints created in response to seventh dimensional musical notes are what you know as 'DNA'.

These 'DNA strands' are living intelligence structures and look just like the mushroom spores. This is a challenge for many individuals to understand, but upon your planet all things stemmed from either the mushroom spore or the DNA strand. That which 'landed' upon your planet (they actually arrived as light codes) were the precursors for all of organic creation, life and matter. However, the light codes from the antimatter reality (or outside of your planetary atmosphere) were only one part of the creational process. The other part were naturally forming organisms that were created upon your planet.

Your Bible, in the Genesis chapter, speaks of the 'sons of God' seeing the 'daughters of men' and together 'children' were born.

This refers to the cosmic organisms upon your planet (daughters of men, as in the naturally forming planetary life structures) coming together with the DNA strands (sons) of the cosmos (God).

So we could show this merge/marriage in five different ways:

1) Cosmos and planet

2) Antimatter and matter

3) Masculine force with feminine force

4) Extraterrestrial with human

5) God's sons with men's daughters

The negative/feminine polarity of planetary consciousness and its living plasma organisms coming together as a fusion with the positive/masculine polarity of cosmic consciousness and its living plasma DNA structures.

The planetary organisms were living consciousness receivers (a blank slate, full of creational energy waiting to receive the blueprints).

The cosmic DNA is a plasmic light (liquid light) containing memory and information. This is that which 'gives', as in 'the giver of light'.

When the cosmic consciousness (the male giving force) moved into a fusion with the planetary consciousness (the female receiving force), then the union creates. The 'creator' and the 'creatrix' energies create the 'spark of life' (the child).

The child is 'that which houses the DNA'.

So many different life forms were created from the original cosmic and planetary plasmic light union.

This creational journey is also explained in our previous transmission *Divine Architecture and the Starseed Template* in the chapter entitled 'The Fall'.

This information speaks of this creational act as light transference upon the hominid beings upon the Earth at that time. This is the same creational aspect we present here. There is no 'time' within the antimatter reality.

Extraterrestrial races mirror and replicate the creational process through genetic manipulation, gene splicing, cloning, copying and light transference. Different extraterrestrials have different methods of doing this and different technology.

You do this when you as male 'give' the information through liquid light transference to the female (who receives).

There are many religious scholars throughout your history who have sought to discover who these 'sons of God' and 'daughters of men' were. Layers and layers of metaphor have been presented and, as we have said, 'metaphor' does not mean that something does not exist. Metaphors are formed in matter as well as in idea, and thought for matter is created from thought.

We present to you the 'highest' or 'deepest' metaphor within that fractal layer that our conduit is currently able to understand. For those amongst you with a physics background, the clue to creation lies here in the word 'fusion'.

So the 'cosmic consciousness' came in through plasmic light, memory and information as pure DNA intelligence. When merged with the planetary organisms, then together the female and the male, which are precursors to life, created life as matter.

Where therefore does this leave mushrooms? As we have said, the mushroom 'spores' came in to your reality on a different stream. The mushroom spores are also a form of memory and information, they contain the instructions for the blueprints for reality from the sixth dimensional level. These 'mushrooms' that grew from these spores were provided for you as 'cosmic keys' for the unlocking of information. They are highly intelligent beings in their own right and wherever DNA 'lands', then so too do the mushroom spores.

They are a 'back up plan' if you will. If your own memory systems do not come online spontaneously then, through synchronicity, you are led to the mushrooms. They carry the 'code' or 'template' for creation. This code is presented in 'real time' (just like the memories within your DNA), coming online in the way that is explained within the 'Superhero Program' chapter of *Divine Architecture and the Starseed Template*.

This information and knowledge is there within a great many different plants (trees, shrubs, flowers, vegetables, fruits and herbs). The mushroom is a complete copy of this information system. It is your 'starseed ascension back up system' if you will.

If you are having problems with memory, the eating of these mushrooms will deliver to you that which is 'cosmic memory'.

This is the same substance as 'blue starphire' but instead of it acting as a precursor to your own triggering, it is the fully-formed 'ascension code' or 'reality code' in and of itself. These mushrooms are neon glowing organisms. Within your body, when consumed, they become pure activated plasmic light. They are luminescent and glow with all the colours of the rainbow, depending on which mushroom you consume.

They also glow with light information that is outside of your colour spectrum on your planet. Different mushrooms hold different codes and different colours.

Whilst in the times of Atlantis they relied on 'crystal technology', the Lemurians used 'plant technology' and especially 'mushroom technology'.

The mushrooms grown at that time were much, much larger than you currently have upon your planet. They were as large as some of your trees are. Rings of mushrooms would together create a stargate or portal where the Lemurians could pass from one dimension to another or jump between harmonics within dimensions. Your old tales of fairy rings have stemmed from this Lemurian truth, being guarded consciously throughout indigenous and especially Celtic tribes.

Lemurians could also break off a piece of the mushroom to consume raw. Each mushroom would hold different coordinates for different 'places' or 'consciousness vortices' (better explained as 'reality domains' within harmonic realities within dimensions). Your story of *Alice in Wonderland* gives to you the catalystic memory clue of this mushroom technology through Alice eating the piece of mushroom to make her smaller or taller. This channelled information, downloaded through the author, is full of clues to reality and holds many catalystic triggers for creation, expansion, enlightenment and ascension.[6]

When it comes to your current now, today reality, many of the exotic and intelligent original mushrooms as the 'backup

---

6   "Alice in Wonderland" (1865) by Lewis Carroll

memory matrices' are not available to you. However, they each hold codes in their own right. The mushrooms you know as 'magic mushrooms' and 'medicinal mushrooms' provide their own codes. The ones containing active psilocybin may certainly be too much for the sensitive starseed, and are to be used magickally and as a vision questing tool. One does not need to consume these beings (and they *are* beings) on a regular bases as this would move one into 'burn out.' (Slow and steady, the tortoise wins the race.)

Medicinal mushrooms may also be too much for very sensitive starseeds, so consume these in small quantities until you are used to them. They are 'reflective' (neon and luminescent) and they reflect 'all that you are'. You indeed 'see yourself' when they are consumed. Be sure you are in a place of self-love, self-confidence or self-awareness when consuming these (or be ready to step into that).

As a sensitive individual, these can trigger extensive and continuous downloads. If you are already sensitive, you will be already accessing this 'multiple download experience' or multidimensional consciousness. So make sure, as we have said, that you work with small amounts of these as you assimilate their energies.

These are the 'plant teachers' which come in many forms. We refer to these specifically as the 'mushroom masters'.

These mushroom masters are starseeds like you (seeded from the stars) and if you are truly looking for 'extraterrestrials', then you will realise they have been right alongside you all this time in the form of mushrooms.

Indeed *all* mushrooms and fungi have stemmed from the original substance we call 'spores' that were seeded upon your planet at the same time as DNA.

Within the 'inner Earth' kingdoms, these mushrooms are vast and are much closer to the mushrooms of the Lemurian times. They glow with neon brightness and are luminous, bioluminescent, 'glow in the dark' entities. You are each attracted to and fascinated with that which 'glows in the dark', especially when you are children. This is because you intrinsically know that these luminous mushrooms hold the 'backup memory systems' for creation and are the 'mushroom masters'.

These luminescent mushrooms not only provide the backup matrices of reality knowledge and information in real time, but also possess substances that can create healing on many levels. They also hold 'immortality codes' which you would translate as 'longevity'. Yet immortality codes are a fully mapped version of the retaining of memory. They are indeed powerful little tools for stargate ascension.

As we have said, some of these are edible for humans and others are not (and are toxic). So be sure to discover within your personal research, journey of information gathering and cross referencing (due diligence) before consuming them.

The mushrooms you gather from your stores, shops and farms hold many beneficial compounds. Whilst they may not trigger you into the full backup memory system, they do work to give you unique dietary nutrients that will assist you as you move into health and balance.

Why do you say 'beyond Atlantis'? What does this mean?

We use this in the context of 'before' Atlantis, as in 'further back' in your history. This takes you to the Lemurian times. Or what we may more accurately term the 'Lemurian consciousness'.

You said Atlantis occurred 'after the fall'. Was Lemuria before the fall?

The fall took place in the time period we call 'Lemuria'. This is known also as 'Original Earth', 'Nirvana', 'Neverland', 'Paradise', 'Utopia' (translated to some as 'Urantia') or 'Eden'.

We refer to this time period as 'Lemuria', yet we could say there were/are (remember Lemuria is now) three stages to Lemuria.

1) Before the fall.

2) During the fall.

3) After the fall.

These three stages took thousands and thousands of years. It would take many lifetimes to present to you the differences in these stages, but in a few words we can say:

1) Before the fall, Lemuria was a fifth dimensional reality. Beings could pass through solid matter, breathe underwater, live without food, grow wings and fly. They could communicate telepathically, live as long as they pleased within an incarnation, choose future incarnations and remember everything from their 'previous' ones. Multidimensional awareness was experienced and they all knew they were part of one another. They followed and lived by the principles of 'the Law of One'.

2) The Lemurian individuals became denser and denser, descending further and further into matter. They phased in and out of their 'light bodies' and their 'physical bodies'. Most Lemurians were excited and joyful for this experience, for they retained the knowledge and memory of why the fall was occurring. The further they fell, the more their memories diminished and eventually they forgot the reasons for the fall. They began to see themselves and one another as separate, but still retained the inner knowing of oneness and harmonious living. A few retained the abilities of telepathy, passing through solid matter and breathing underwater (the starseeds of your today). These are the 'wandering souls' who experience multiple realities simultaneously yet retain individual presence. These are the rainbow warriors, these are you!

3) Third dimensional existence. Living in tribal community and with harmony with the planet. Mostly spiritually aware, loving, plant eaters. Eventually, some beginning to consume animal flesh which then took them fully into separation and gave some of them a 'warlike' or 'battle' mentality. This began the 'downfall' of the Lemurian races.

However, there was no 'downfall'. For the Lemurian race still exists today within you, dear starseeds, who either chose to return to other planetary systems for their incarnations, became part of the group mind Logos consciousness or incarnated within Atlantis and began a 'multiple incarnational' journey (linear expression of memory imprints and the integration of morphogenetic imprinting).

Each of you exist now, in your today moment at the time of this transmission, the year is 2019.

Some of you are newborn babies, some are children and many of you are adults. It matters not which time period you arrive at this information, for there is no time within the higher consciousness and Lemuria lives on.

So within this transmission we have taken you, through catalysing memory triggering 'beyond Atlantis', into your Lemurian roots within your soul/solar memory. Yes, your sun contains memory codes which you access through the 'hormone' you call 'vitamin D' - found within the mushroom masters! Many clues, many codes!

Wherever these catalysing triggers may take you, know that you are never alone on your cosmic journey of ascension. Allow inspiration, excitement, knowing and joy of life to permeate your very being. For these are the emotions needed for accelerated or stargate ascension.

We remain your humble servants, messengers of the divine, angels/angles of geometric light. It is our absolute honour to serve you at this time through our conduit, Magenta Pixie, who walks the journey with you.

We remain, within 'real time' flow as we continue to download our transmissions to guide and assist you through the ascension cycle into planetary and galactic completion. From our divine heartphire centre to your collective open hearts.

We are the White Winged Collective Consciousness of Nine

13: The Golden Chalice

As you enter the state you know as meditation, imagine, if you will, that you are standing in a beautiful garden.

The garden is full of the most beautiful green grass, tall trees and colourful flowers.

It is a place of calm and serenity and although this place is new to you, on some level it feels familiar, as if you have been here before.

It feels safe.

You feel as though this place is an aspect of your true home.

As you take in the natural breathtaking beauty of this garden, you notice over in the far right corner what looks like an entrance to a cave.

This is no ordinary cave, you notice, but a cave made of the purest brightest blue crystal.

It truly is breathtaking.

You notice how the sun shines upon the crystal blue of the cave and you feel somehow this cave is beckoning to you, calling you forward.

You start to walk towards the entrance to the cave.

When you arrive at the cave entrance, you notice it is even more beautiful close up.

Although the cave is made of this glorious bright blue crystal, there are tiny turquoise crystals and clear diamonds inside the blue crystal all around the mouth of the cave.

The feeling here is one of cleansing, purging and rebirthing.

You walk inside.

Natural sunlight fills the cave as you walk inside.

Even though there does not seem any way for the sun to shine, it does shine, and the view is one of breathtaking beauty.

The feel within the cave is of calm, peace, serenity and safety.

You notice a small pool of crystal clear water.

The water has a blue colour to it, as the sunlight reflects from the blue crystal ceiling of the cave.

There is a golden goblet on the side of the rock pool.

It is an ancient magic chalice of the purest gold.

You pick up the chalice and look inside, and you notice some grey liquid sitting at the bottom of the chalice.

As soon as you see this grey liquid, you know instantly that it is energy you have been holding on to, energy from past romantic relationships and indeed present romantic relationships if they no longer serve you.

You know that this energy is physical, and you know it is now time to let it go, to wash it away, to free yourself.

You wash the golden chalice in the clear blue water.

After washing the chalice in the beautiful water, you once again look inside.

Now you see a light brown liquid inside the chalice.

You know instantly that this is energy from past romantic relationships and indeed present romantic relationships that no longer serve you.

You know that this energy is emotional, and that it is now time to cleanse this emotional energy away that you have been holding on to.

You wash the golden chalice in the crystal clear blue water.

After washing the chalice in the rock pool, you look inside once more and see a dark red fluid.

You instantly know that this is energy left over from past romantic relationships and from present romantic relationships that no longer serve you.

You know deep inside that it is time to free the mind and the thoughts from these energies you have been holding on to, and you wash the golden chalice a third time in the water of the pool.

Once more you look inside the chalice, and you see a cloudy blue liquid.

You know that this is the spiritual energy that you have been holding on to from past romantic relationships and from present romantic relationships that no longer serve you.

You know that it is time to release these connections and ties, and move beyond karma and enforced reincarnation into choice - conscious choice about your own soul trajectory.

You wash the golden chalice in the clear blue waters of the rock pool.

You look inside the chalice and your heart is filled with joy.

Every cell in your body sings with the freedom and the release of the purging that has just taken place.

The vessel no longer contains energy remnants from past romantic relationships and present romantic relationships that no longer serve you.

The chalice is empty, save for the glint of pure gold.

The vessel is now pure, purged and clear.

You know that the only energy it will now contain is your own energy, pure energy of choice and the energy of conscious relationships with those who mirror all that is you.

You know that you can transmute the energy from the like-minded conscious romantic relationship within the natural cyclical flow that abounds through the earth.

You are free to begin again, a fresh page within new romantic relationships that fit your energy frequency and that are part of your blueprint.

This may be an upgrade of your present relationship, as the twin flame potentials are birthed between you.

Or it may be a new meeting that shall lead to the sacred handfasting or the divine marriage in physical form.

Whatever may be the journey from now, you know you are free, purged, released, unburdened, fresh and whole.

The blue crystal cave has called you and you have been cleansed.

As you replace the golden chalice upon the rock and leave the crystal blue cave, you know you have been through a rebirthing process and indeed you feel reborn.

Now in the garden are butterflies, butterflies everywhere of every colour and of such beauty.

They fly before you and around you.

They land on the grass, the trees and the flowers.

They are so beautiful and the mere sight of them fills your heart with wonder and with joy.

When it is time to leave the garden, you know instinctively that you can return here any time you desire, for this place is yours.

It has been found by you, the secret garden and the crystal blue caves of purging, cleansing, rebirthing and transformation.

You return to your physical body, retaining the fresh new feeling of having been reborn.

You feel happiness, joy and peace and you become aware of your physical body.

You become aware of your feet, your legs, your torso, arms, neck and head.

You stretch or move or do whatever is comfortable.

Moving out of the state you know as 'meditation', you allow your awareness to move back into the physical dimension and the waking experience, feeling refreshed, rejuvenated, balanced and clear.

Enjoy this book?

Masters of the Matrix

Divine Architecture and the Starseed Template

The Infinite Helix and the Emerald Flame

The Black Box Programme and the Rose Gold Flame as Antidote

"Look no further, all is explained in this book, encapsulating all religious texts and then explaining further. All answers are given and accessible by all, it only takes an open heart of unconditional love and you too can have all the secrets of all realities revealed to you."

Amazon customer review of *The Infinite Helix and the Emerald Flame*

Made in the USA
Coppell, TX
12 February 2021

50285410R00100